The Timeless Home

Dominic Bradbury

The Timeless Home

James Gorst Architects

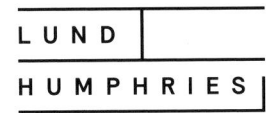

LUND HUMPHRIES

First published in 2019 by Lund Humphries

Lund Humphries
Office 3, Book House
261A City Road
London EC1V 1JX
UK

www.lundhumphries.com

The Timeless Home: James Gorst Architects ©
Dominic Bradbury and James Gorst Architects, 2019.
All rights reserved

ISBN: 978-1-84822-271-7

A Cataloguing-in-Publication record for this book is available from the British Library

All rights reserved. No part of this publication may be reproduced, stored in a retrieval system or transmitted in any form or by any means, electrical, mechanical or otherwise, without first seeking the permission of the copyright owners and publishers. Every effort has been made to seek permission to reproduce the images in this book. Any omissions are entirely unintentional, and details should be addressed to the publishers.

Dominic Bradbury has asserted his right under the Copyright, Designs and Patent Act, 1988, to be identified as the Author of this Work.

Copy edited by Julie Gunz
Designed by Myfanwy Vernon-Hunt, this-side.co.uk
Set in Austin and Graphik
Printed in Italy

Front cover
Fulford Farm

Page 2
Fulford Farm

Right
Hannington Farm from the first floor entrance hall landing to the cantilevered bedroom gallery.

Contents

7	Foreword by James Gorst
23	Introduction

Rural Estates
31	Fulford Farm
43	Hannington Farm

Houses
59	Whithurst Lodge
65	Glen View
73	Leaf House
79	Brick House
85	Sandpipers

Reinventions and Adaptations
99	Wakelins
109	Watergate
117	Downs House
125	Hurworth House
133	House of Detention

Interiors and Furniture
143	Shelley Court
151	Eaton Square, Apartment One
157	Eaton Square, Apartment Two
163	South Audley Street
169	Lamb's Conduit Street

176	Acknowledgements and Chronology

Foreword

James Gorst

The history of western architecture is pre-eminently the history of two building types – the house and the church. The sacred and the profane. In the crucible of these two genres we see the evolution of architectural development as changing functional imperatives are addressed through formal and spatial experimentation.

As architectural practice unfolded the architects of the house were, like the architects of the church, adept in addressing both changing liturgical requirements and changing ways of living. This has been the case from Alberti to Lutyens, from Palladio to Le Corbusier. The challenge in architecture, regardless of building type, is to create a formal and spatial experience that surprises, astonishes and delights.

This may seem a vaunting ambition but it is nevertheless the motivation for all serious architects. In our practice over the last 30 years we have drunk deep from the spring of history and have looked always to achieve the highest standards – to work towards a poetic expression in which volume and space, form and geometry, and materiality and light synthesise into an architecture of calm and sensual beauty.

Beginnings

My first experience of the immanence of architecture, of its potential to hold back time and transport the imagination, came as a boy aged 6 or 7 in a Tudor threshing barn in the Suffolk farming village in which I grew up. I had been playing with my childhood companions Duncan, the doctor's son and Peter, the farmer's son. We had been messing around on the farm amongst the sheds and in the stack yard. All the men were up on the fields by the Hyde wood, gathering in the harvest. The farm and its buildings were free for our unsupervised inspection and distraction. Our play finally took us to the great thatched, black pitch-tarred threshing barn.

Like entering a church or cinema in the hot midday, the abrupt actinic switch from the sharp brightness outside to the shuttered dark of the silent interior was a dramatic, immersive experience, causing us to pause. My companions soon peeled away, distracted by fresh urgent imperatives. I remained and as my eyes slowly adjusted I began to make out the immense volume of the barn articulated by its cobweb-laced oak frame. From a single high casement a shaft of dazzling sunlight scorched down to the dusty floor, illuminating dancing motes suspended in mid-air. The chiaroscuro of this dark and silent space might have been unsettling to my childhood self. In fact, it was deeply reassuring and restful. Around me I made out the scattered and discarded implements of a pre-mechanised age of farming: weather-worn oaken yokes smoothed and reshaped by shire horses' shoulders, broken pitch forks, coils of rope, rusted buckets, toothless wooden rakes, a scattering of straw bales like abandoned installations. Only one draught horse remained working on the farm now – a Suffolk Punch. Blue Fordson tractors had replaced the rest and the threshing itself was now done by the combine harvester up on the field as it scythed through the wheat. Now, decades on, the barn remains in name only. Its thatched roof has been replaced by imitation slates, its oak frame and cobwebs concealed beneath plasterboard partitions, its noble integrity sacrificed to the demands of residential use. New life for old buildings.

The piercing shaft of light, a beloved trope of Baroque religious art, symbolises the illumination of divine grace. That distant experience in the abandoned threshing barn, recollected now in tranquillity, was my profane analogue and the moment of my inadvertent architectural epiphany. I left the barn and went looking for Duncan and Peter. Life goes on.

Our house was across the road from the barn. My father became chief planning officer in 1952, when I was two. He purchased an acre of land from Mr Kemp fronting onto the village green with three mature limes, a chestnut by the gate and a sycamore to the rear. A friend of his, Eric Sandon, author of the definitive but unindexed guide to Suffolk domestic architecture, designed a new house for us of 1500 square feet, just within the established post-war constraints of rationing. It was a modernist bungalow with large picture-frame windows that birds crashed into, a fitted kitchen with formica tops, flush doors, splayed skirtings, fabrics by Robin and Lucienne Day, furniture by Ercol and G plan and surprisingly a loggia. It cost £4000 to build. There were three bedrooms and just one bathroom and as I and my three brothers grew larger the house began to seem smaller, barely able to contain us both physically or emotionally.

My father, charismatic and unpredictable, was the undisputed patriarch of this cramped affair. Whilst in later life he became increasingly conservative, I think for him the 1950s must have been an invigorating time. He had had a good war, rising from a non-commissioned volunteer to becoming a major on Montgomery's staff. On being demobbed he went on to qualify as a civil engineer and then to become one of the first of the new planning officers following the 1947 Town and Country Planning Act. The arrival of the Beveridge reforms, along with the chance to rebuild our towns and cities with decent housing and transport, inspired his generation of planners with a utopian zeal and our low-slung modern bungalow, named without irony after South Stack – a towering lighthouse off the coast of Anglesea – was for him all a part of his commitment to a new non-deferential social order. This really was his symbolic lighthouse; a modernist beacon. But while the house symbolised his optimism, his personal situation was existentially more complex, his place in society more tenuous. Good looking, tall, charismatic and clever he charmed the members of the gentry and the aristocracy that filled the chairs of the West Suffolk County Council planning committee in the mid 1960s. What a roll call – Doris Pleydell Bouverie, the Marchioness of Bristol, Sir Joshua Rowley, Sir George Falconer and so on and so on. Their equal in charm and perhaps superior in intellect, there would on occasion be an invitation for lunch, *noblesse oblige*, but never of course any suggestion of dinner. He was drawn dangerously like a moth towards these people and probably yearned for some greater intimacy, but he knew the score. At the same time he had no real common ground with the farmers and shopkeepers of Bury St Edmunds so he was alone without any real social hinterland and his loneliness and frustration were acted out in the 1500 square feet of our family home.

Forty-three years later he died in the house he had built. He died at midnight. My mother held his lifeless body until the morning came. We had all left home long before. The house was sold and altered and extended beyond recognition – like the barn. The light had gone out on South Stack, but it remains in me and I can summon it back at will in every detail, pattern and fibre.

In the 1960s, in my teens, I began to hang out with boys and girls whose parents lived in large old houses – Georgian or Tudor – in the surrounding villages. They went away during term time to expensive boarding schools. I was seduced by their style and nonchalance, by the parties and the houses filled with paintings and books. These old farm houses, manors and rectories were the *mise en scène* of the glamorous parents and children who lived within – or so I erroneously thought. I would return home to the low ceilings, flush doors, splayed skirtings and plain details of our home in which ornament was crime and think wistfully about sash windows, marble fire surrounds, stone paved halls and panelled shutters. I didn't want egalitarian modernism, I wanted the house style of the *ancien régime* and this was all very conflicting personally because in my mind, in the late 1960s, I was a pot smoking, progressive anti-establishment radical who championed the oppressed – simultaneously social climber and class warrior. Beyond the self-delusion, unbeknownst to me, I was beginning to act out a parallel enslaving narrative to my father's.

Pages 6–7
Skylights over the swimming pool at Hannington Farm.

One afternoon, having tea in the garden, my mother, a woman who was as insightful as my father was intemperate, intimated in a kindly and sorrowful way that I had perhaps become embarrassed by my home and my family. I was mortified by the partial truth behind her observation and the implied betrayal of the charge. These teenage insecurities around identity and social class have a toxically lingering effect on personality and never really go away. However much we bury them in a trunk in the darkest corner of the basement we know they are still there, diminishing us and spoiling things.

I mention this because in some way throughout 35 years of restlessly buying and selling houses for myself I have been looking to cloak my own uncertainties around class and identity in the camouflage of property, and while I've made lots of houses I'm not sure I've ever made a home of my own as my father did. I think I yearn for it but at the same time the legacy of claustrophobic intensity, overbearing paternal constraint and sibling rivalry has made it hard for me to want replicate it.

In every dream home a heartache

So, I design houses for a living and occasionally the charge is levelled that they don't make homes. I think this is wrong, but I understand the charge. I don't work with the familiar components of the classical or vernacular house in the manner of the large-volume house builders. Their houses reference past traditions in ways that reassure their clients – they are buying a house, preferably detached, which will become a home. It is an industrialised and mass-produced version of traditional hand-built vernacular forms – a fake architecture legitimised through endless ubiquitous repetition. These counterfeit houses become synonymous with the aspirational values of independence and success. The volume house builder understands this and satisfies his market.

However, architects who use the house as a means of architectural expression are doing something more complicated. We are constrained by budget, context and brief to design a building that will fit within those parameters. But ultimately we are not designing for the client who finances the project but for ourselves and for the judgement of our peers. We try to please the client but subversively we are engaged in our own particular and parallel agenda – to add a footnote to the story of the house. Like suburban explorers we take buses, planes and trains to seek out the illustrious houses of the past in remote locations to pay homage and draw inspiration – to Villa Tugendhat in Brno, to Villa Savoye in Poissy, to the suburbs of Prague to see Villa Muller by Adolf Loos, to Chicago to see the Robie House, to the Ticino to see the early houses of Mario Botta, to Pennsylvania to see Fallingwater.

In my search for an architecture of pure abstract form I am pitched against the scale and the quotidian requirements of the private house – the need for front doors, back doors, so many bedrooms and so many bathrooms and so many other rooms all wanting windows that punctuate and interrupt the rhythmic sweep of surface and the play of abstract sculptural form that larger institutional building types can permit. I suppose in this way I am trying to depersonalise and undomesticate the house – to give it a greater scale and a more enigmatic, less identifiable presence. Despite these ambivalent attitudes, and perhaps the desire to work on buildings of a larger, more public scale, I remain in thrall to the challenge of combining formal architectonic invention within the challenges and constraints of the private house. And what a privilege it is to design spaces in which people will rest and feel safe, cook meals and share company, listen to music and play, make love and argue, raise families and, of course, live and die. The intimate arena of life. But now it is increasingly not for life. The turbulence of divorce and the restless transience of life today means the settled home and hearth of our forebears has become an aspiration rather than a reality. Often it is chasing the fantasy of the dream home and the future life it betokens that simultaneously sustains and drains the marriage throughout the financial and emotional stress of builders and planners and architects, leaving the dreamers exhausted upon completion. Too much has been sacrificed and put on hold during the process, placing unrealistic expectations on the finished house to fill the void: in every dream home a heartache.

I went up to Cambridge to read Law but, following an hour on the Law of Torts, I decided at lunchtime to change to History. I enjoyed reading History and perhaps would have improved on my 2.1 had I not been distracted by communal living and the twin demands of the counter culture – music and dope. As my third and final year approached I realised that a History degree wasn't going to take me far in mid 1970s Britain – there weren't as many interesting jobs then as there are now – so, with the support of my Local Education Authority, I committed to a further five years of Architecture. This wasn't quite so random: I had originally gone up to Cambridge to read Architecture. I was told to take a portfolio with me for my interview. The night before, lacking a portfolio, I hurriedly traced over some postcards of Snape Maltings that I found lying around. I presented these tracings to Barry Gasson, the Director of Studies at my College who was at the time designing the

Burrell Gallery in Glasgow. He looked at them for a moment, and then looked quizzically at me. 'You've traced these off postcards haven't you'. I agreed and the interview was concluded. A week later the college offered me a place to read Law.

Architecture in the mid 1970s was in retreat. The late flowering baroque bravura of Brutalism was extinguished. Modernism was judged to have failed and the architects were in the dock. With the partial exception of the hi-tech supremacists whose way was not mine, this led to a plethora of eager-to-please sub vernacular buildings dressed reassuringly, whatever their scale, in brick, slate and timber. This collective search for redemption in the eyes of the general public had a dispiriting effect upon architectural education and it was not until the late 1970s, with the writings of Tafuri, Vidler and Frampton and the new works of Stirling and Graves, that things began to seem aesthetically and culturally interesting again. While the built expression of postmodern theory was generally alarmingly awful, its theoretical achievement was to encourage architects to believe once again in the primacy of their pursuit as an art in itself beyond functional imperatives. For me this reconnection to history and to pure architectonic values was all that mattered. Given the times this was probably an illiberal, apolitical and elitist diversion on my part and certainly it led me into the realm of looking for moneyed bourgeois patrons to achieve my aims, something I look back on now with occasional mixed feelings.

Practice

While a student I conformed and attempted to work in the kind of expression of Cambridge modernism – well-behaved and rather Scandinavian – that prevailed at the time. I went through the motions without conviction. I realised I had no understanding at all, even after five years of formal education, of what architecture was about. If this shape, why not another? Where did meaning and authority lie? I see now that this anxiety remains at the heart of the self-criticism of any artistic creation. Eventually out of the uncertainty and equivocation a series of proposals emerge that are consistent and balanced and express formally what one is striving to achieve. This process can be either swift or protracted and there will always be revisions and adjustments.

However, before I was able to produce the majority of the works in this book I needed to forget the appliqué modernism of my Cambridge education and go back to source material. In my final year at Cambridge, I wrote a dissertation on the clubs of St James's. This entailed early morning visits to the clubs in Pall Mall and St James's before members arrived for pre-prandial drinks. Under the sceptical gaze of the staff I penetrated the neoclassical splendour of Brooks's club. The observation and experience of how Henry Holland manipulated the spatial narrative of the club from the narrow, constrained entrance of the porters' lodge into the triple height of the internal staircase hall and thereon to the barrel-vaulted rooms of the *piano nobile* brought home to me for the first time the extent to which the modulation and orchestration of volume was really the main game in architecture. Whilst this formal spatial modulation was organised axially and symmetrically the lessons nevertheless of this visit were absolutely transferable to the non-axial arrangements I later explored with the modern house plan.

In the early 1980s I worked for a couple of years in the offices of two very contrasting architects: Sir Denys Lasdun and John Outram. Lasdun may be said to have turned structure into decoration while Outram did the opposite. I then set up (prematurely) on my own. Following a chance encounter with a university friend in the Nags Head in Covent Garden, I was recklessly instructed to design four shops in Farnworth, Lancashire. Hungry for self-expression I imposed on this humble brief a heroic facade of rusticated columns, four ring arches and bulls-eye windows all in blue engineering bricks surmounted by an overbearing gable of red bricks.

The mock-heroic scheme was a meditation on the industrial architecture of the north and a reverent lament for its decline. This was the early 1980s and the northern landscape seen from the train was one of dereliction and closures. On the day of the first site meeting I was accompanied on the journey by the experienced and phlegmatic engineer who assured me, I think by way of encouragement, that the architect was king. I had no previous experience of running a meeting and no idea of what was required of me in my role as a king. Fortunately, the contractors' site agent, a Chinese Liverpudlian, was a kindly soul who I'm sure detected my inexperience but chose not to expose it. I survived the ordeal intact, which was more than could be said for the building which, when completed and exposed to its first winter, proved to be rather pervious.

Until I received a phone call from my clients' solicitor – 'James, old chap, I'm afraid I've got some rather bad news' – I hadn't realised that architects needed insurance. The next few wintry weeks were spent on the wind- and rain-swept roof hacking open the rear brickwork to my grandly rhetorical and permeable gabled facade. This was an instructive experience. I emerged unscathed and exonerated – cavity trays had not been installed correctly and as drawn. I went out and got some insurance.

Right
Bolton: from profane to sacred – four shops recruited into the Salvation Army.

During this period of solitary working I restored any number of Georgian houses in London that had fallen into disrepair, generally returning them from multiple occupation into family homes. The post-war central London boroughs still bore evidence of bomb-damaged sites amidst rows of dilapidated terraces. The state had focused energy and resources either on the construction of new inner-city estates or in the development of the new towns, leaving the run-down Georgian and Victorian housing stock in the hands of private landlords. In a few short years, from 1981 to 1985, I moved three times, from a mid 19th-century terraced house in Islington to a four-storey house in Barnsbury to a five-storey house in Bloomsbury. Each of the houses had suffered the depredations of time and neglect and each house presented progressively a more exciting challenge – of returning the fabric to its original condition.

In this work, both for myself and for what clients I had, I became familiar with the details of construction and proportion and the proprieties of detailing, from basement to attic, in 18th-century domestic architecture, from simple artisans' dwellings to Class 1 houses. The way all these houses regardless of scale drew from a common lexicon of detailing, decoration and proportion left me continually amazed by the collective genius of the Georgians and the surety of their aesthetic control.

Pie Corner, Bedmond, in 1988, was a distillation of what I had learned and absorbed: a stripped neoclassical meditation on the idealised villa translated into 18th-century Soanian rationalism. Pie Corner, a rather irritating name for a house, was built on a smallish estate of land nestled within the junction of the M1 and the M25, on the fringe of the commuter settlement of Bedmond. With an attractive open prospect to the front framed by woodland and a steep wooded bank to the rear, the house stands alone in a rather compromised rural setting.

Prior to receiving the commission I had spent some time in the Ticino district of Switzerland looking at the Khanian early houses of Mario Botta, which I was greatly inspired by. Initially the house was to be for one of the daughters, a shoe designer, who was open to modernism. However, in a twist of fate which was to realign the direction of my career for a few years to come, she was then substituted as client, for internal family reasons, by the more conservative eldest son, a barrister much in the mould of his eminently conservative father. In this way modernism was put to one side for 15 years and the future took its course.

However, at Pie Corner I was able in a very modest way to put into practice those lessons gleaned from Henry Holland. A narrow entrance hall with Soanian bead and butt panelling to walls and ceiling, followed by a wider, higher ceilinged plastered hall which in turn led into a double-height top-lit galleried octagonal atrium off which, concluding the enfilade, was a fitted library. To the side was a staircase hall with a cantilevered stone stair. The house was built with no general contractor, with the client's mother acting as a rather grand clerk of works marshalling an assortment of subcontractors of varying commitment and enthusiasm. Given the detail of the building – much bead and butt panelling, fitted joinery, bookcasing, bespoke stone floors inlaid with black marble not to mention the cantilevered stone stair with wrought-iron balustrading and a nickel handrail – it was quite an achievement. Two attendant garages with (unofficial) accommodation above stood as framing, sentinel lodges to the main house (a similar device to that used much later at Whithurst Lodge). I received another phone call a while after completion – again an issue with porosity. There was consistency in my early work. This time though I had insurance and despite my endeavours my client felt compelled to sue me, so £3000 was duly deducted from my exiguous fee of £12,000. Another life-affirming lesson. Further anguish was to follow when another architect was engaged to build a flat-roofed extension connecting the lodges to the house, thereby

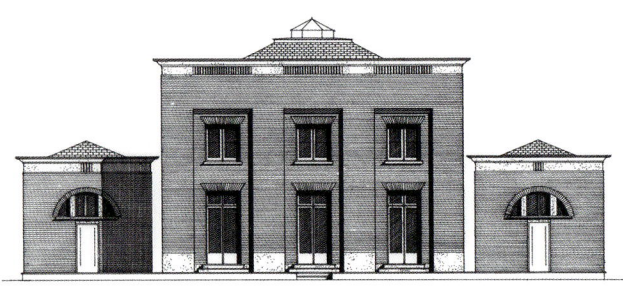

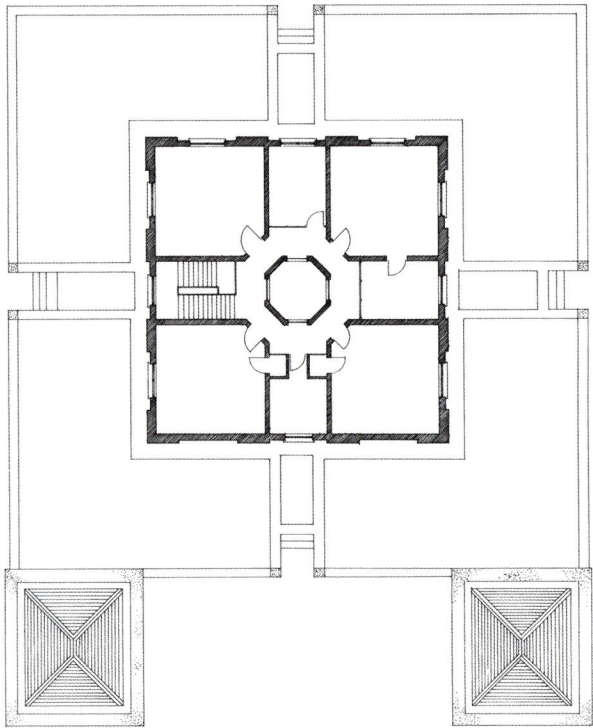

Above
Pie Corner elevation and plan: the centralized villa – the tyranny of geometry.

Right, above
The neoclassical propriety and Soanian sobriety of Pie Corner. The house and its attendant lodges are a vulnerable pastoral setting, threatened by suburban spread and the roar of the M25.

Right
The original entrance elevation – now sadly obscured by insensitive infilling.

Below, right
Gibson House and the new end pavilion to the Gibson Square palace-fronted terrace.

Below, far right
The 'pylonic' corner tower of Gibson House.

eviscerating the central conceit of the design – the relationship of major to minor, the parts to the whole.

Around this time, while living in the first of my three north London houses, no.4 Rees Street, I used occasionally to take a drink at the nearby Duke of York. On one visit I was drawn aside by George, the stuttering landlord, who wondered if I would be interested in designing some houses for a fire-damaged site of his on the corner of Gibson Square and Liverpool Road. I was naturally eager to please and designed eight flats and two houses. The scheme completed the palace-fronted terrace to Gibson Square with the two houses forming the un-built northern pavilion and, for the first time, symmetrically balancing the original composition. The eight flats formed Gibson House, described by Charles Jencks in his 1991 *Post-Modern Triumphs in London* as 'an exceptional culmination of a Georgian terrace which transforms the Neo-Classical language in subtle ways starting with the tapered 'Egyptian' light-house pylons at the entrance, continuing up to the cantilevered horizontals of the balconies and doors and then the attic floor treated as a cross between early Wright and Egyptian. The proportional relationship of brick to stucco and twin pavilions to set back is strong, obvious and sensible. This is urbane Post-Modernism in its most civil mode.' I'm not sure I could have put it better and I'm sure it was just what George was looking for.

Following more refurbishments and a bellyful of clients who saw me simply as a conduit for their magazine-derived inspirations, I decided in 1992 to jack in architecture as a lost cause, sell our house in Doughty Street and escape back to the fresh air of my Suffolk roots. I felt that I'd become narrowly defined as a classicist but felt no ideological commitment to the new classicism and the young fogeys who propounded the cause. I wanted to do work that was fresh and contemporary and rid myself of the antiquarian straitjacket I'd got into. I looked on in envy and despair at the progressive work of my contemporaries but couldn't see how to be part of it. How had I got into this? Was this the revenge of the rectory?

So I broke free and sold up, but how did I break free? By buying a semi-derelict Tudor and Georgian house in the middle of Lavenham, a medieval village in Suffolk. My first wife Sarah and I set about restoring it with me as the labourer working with a carpenter, a roofer and an electrician. The liberation from clients and the absorption in the slow, careful and authentic

restoration of this beautiful old house made this on one level a very happy and fulfilling experience. I made plans to become a probation worker and do something more socially engaged with my life but shortly before the interview with the Home Office the phone rang, and I got drawn back to London and architecture. I resolved to do no more work in a classical style. I had learnt from classical architecture but saw no profit in making a life of its replication – although, as it turns out, that is where the profit is, the English being generally unconvinced by modernism even now.

I moved between my house in Lamb's Conduit Street, in which I once again set up an office, and Lavenham for long weekends with the family. However, having found the perfect house I engineered the break-up of the home – Sarah and I separated and the dream house was sold. The bewilderment at the destruction I had caused remains, as does the memory of walking through the empty rooms we had so lovingly brought back to life, the contents stacked in boxes awaiting the removal van's arrival.

I was offered by a loyal client the chance to build a new house in Chelsea on a prominent corner site in Glebe Place. This was around the corner from a Voysey house and diagonally opposite a house by Philip Webb in which the brilliant Stanley Kubrick directed his last film *Eyes Wide Shut* with the tall Nicole Kidman and the hard-to-love Tom Cruise. For these contextual reasons I decided to design the house as a homage to the indigenous Arts and Crafts tradition. I would have essayed a contemporary design but there was no appetite for modernism in Kensington and Chelsea in the mid 1990s, so I immersed myself in this uniquely British idiom, exploiting to the full the formal and material opportunities that the style provides – plain oak and painted panelled wainscoting, bronze casements with leaded lights, base bed Portland stone floors, architectural joinery, barrel-vaulted ceilings, clay peg tiles, bath stone, pebble dash, exposed oak trusses – in short the whole nine yards. Nearing completion my kind and glamorous client suffered a serious reverse and the consequent unravelling of his life. It looked as if the contractor and I would remain unpaid,

Above, left
Conservatives would have voted out a modern house in Glebe Place in the mid-1990s so instead a respectful *homage* to the great English fiction of the Arts and Crafts was followed and embraced.

Above, centre
West staircase window of Glebe Place house. Bath stone, pebble dash, bronze casements, leaded lights, clay peg tiles – all the usual Arts and Crafts suspects.

Above, right
The central galleried staircase hall looking towards the courtyard. Good materials (including Portland stone, English oak and painted panelling) and good workmanship from contractors R. Durtnell and Sons, founded in 1591.

Below, left
A quirky house in Poundbury.

Below, right
A nursing home in the middle of Poundbury.

our debts unsecured, with the property passing into the hands of some very dissatisfied and not over-particular creditors. The contractor however, sought and secured a Mareva injunction, freezing the assets until we were paid. The unfinished house was then acquired by my client's wife's father, a diminutive and immaculate Belgian plastic surgeon not unlike Hercule Poirot, who was almost as dissatisfied with his son-in-law as were his other creditors. We finished the house to the full original specification, all parties were paid in full and the wealthy plastic surgeon became richer still.

Glebe Place was featured in *Perspectives* magazine, then edited by the late Giles Worsley. Giles became a friend and supporter and the coverage of Glebe Place led to further skirmishes with Arts and Crafts idioms in the design of a large nursing home in the centre of Poundbury for the Duchy of Cornwall. Whilst designing the nursing home I managed to slip through a couple of pleasingly perverse detached houses before a parting of the ways with the Poundbury hierarchy.

However, I was as loath to become known as a practitioner of ersatz Arts and Crafts as I had been to be known as a neoclassicist ten years earlier. And so, with both genres investigated and considered, I was finally presented with the opportunity to design a contemporary non-historicist standalone house. The opportunity came generously from Richard Taylor and his partner Rick Englert, who asked for a tile-hung lodge in the Sussex vernacular and got nothing remotely resembling it (Whithurst Lodge, see page 59).

Though stylistically antithetical the Lodge has in common with Pie Corner a plan in which the disparate functions of the house are subjugated to the tyranny of an imposed symmetry. To the modernist this may well be apostasy and it is generally the case in all the houses I have designed thereafter that the plan and section and the programme of movement through the house have been the drivers of the design, with the elevations following thereon. The Lodge was inspired by a holiday in Finland searching out the work of Alvar

Aalto. Gazing out on long train journeys at the unchanging monotony of endless dark and lifeless pine forests relieved only by sporadic settlements, these moments of human habitation lived in the forest took on an intense significance and fascination: a Tsarist railway station, children playing in a meadow of wild flowers, neatly stacked log piles, red houses with white casements and heavy browed eaves. Typically the houses were built against the dark forest with an open meadow to the front. The Lodge offered just such a possibility with an established stand of deciduous trees to the rear and parkland to the fore. These Finnish houses occupied a symbolic threshold between light and dark, diurnal and nocturnal, mystery and reason, the conscious and the subconscious. Following this conceit, the original intention for the Lodge was a closed and un-fenestrated first floor atop a fully glazed and transparent ground floor. The first-floor bedrooms were to be illuminated by filtered light from the longitudinal skylight passing through opaque 'japanese' screen partitions. This was the forest, the land of dreams and the unconscious. On waking and descending one re-entered the diurnal world with the landscape as decoration. Richard and Rick were largely supportive of this idea, but felt, not unreasonably, that a couple of windows might be, from their point of view, an improvement.

Simultaneously I was presented with the opportunity to design a new rear extension to Giles and Joanna Worsley's house in Cambridge Gardens, Notting Hill. The austere rear elevation of London stock bricks was a receptive background for a simple composition of projecting volumes.

A few years before working on the Lodge, I carried out the alteration and refurbishment of a mansion block apartment, Shelley Court in Tite Street, Chelsea (see page 143). The organisation of the apartment was changed from the privacy obsessed English mode of individual sequestered rooms off corridors to a more 19th-century European model in which an enfilade of rooms formed a *promenade architecturale* through the space. The uninspired Edwardian detailing was stripped and the deracinated apartment rebuilt in a sober, high bourgeois Loosian manner to produce an interior that was, in Baudelaire's words, *luxe, calme et volupte*, including book-matched mahogany veneers, a bedroom in sapele pommele, silk curtains, bespoke handmade rugs, an entrance hall in Nero Portoro marble, fabric-covered walls, parquet floors. Into this we designed a number of pieces of furniture – side tables, a drinks cabinet, a desk, a chest of drawers, bedside tables – in various veneers from burr walnut to sapele all made by master joiners and cabinet makers in deepest Norfolk.

Above
Whithurst Lodge.

Right
Cambridge Gardens: an austere extension to the undecorated rear facade of a terraced house in Notting Hill, much loved by Gorst's client, the late Giles Worsley.

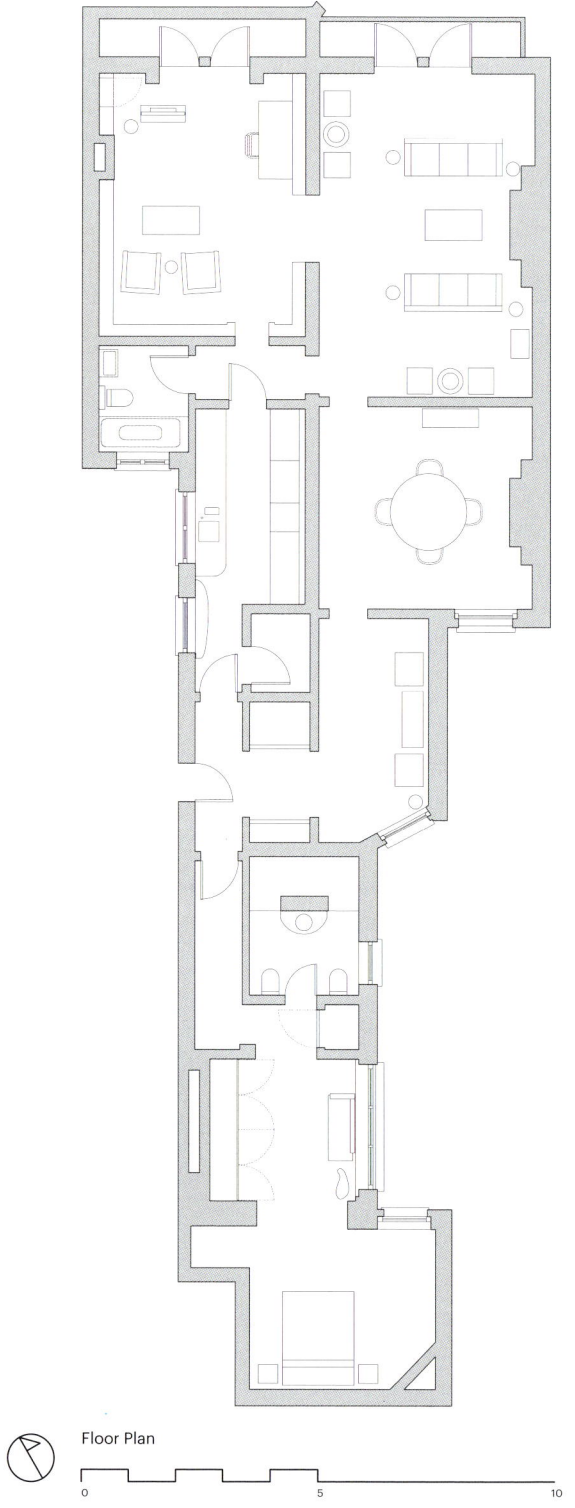

Floor Plan

Opposite, far left
The Shelley Court apartment entrance hall. Mahogany rat's tail veneers after Adolf Loos, a chair by Philippe Hurel, a telephone table by James Gorst Architects and a painting by Ivon Hitchens.

Opposite Left
The reconfigured apartment. The Edwardian obsession with corridors and privacy substituted for a more European model in which a succession of rooms follow one from another providing a *promenade architecturale*.

Above
A drinks cabinet by James Gorst Architects in burr walnut.

These pieces of furniture extended the atmosphere of the architecture into the contained *objets* within. This interior was not only engrossing in the opportunities it provided to consider colour, fabric, texture, atmosphere and history but it also sparked an enduring fascination on my part in the complex challenge of an approach to interior decoration that looked beyond the modish tropes and whimsies of the currently fashionable.

My client and patron Richard Morris, for whom we did the Ruhlmann-inspired apartment at Shelley Court (see page 143), then purchased Wakelins (see page 99), an ancient and adulterated farmhouse near Newmarket, Suffolk. Over two and a half very happy years we rebuilt with local master builders the house and its adjacent barn and added on a two-storey timber frame extension clad in scalloped oak boards. Our role again extended to the furnishing and decoration of the house from the bed linen to the tableware, with many purpose-made items designed by the office – desks, tables and chairs.

In complete contrast to the veneered polish of Shelley Court, Wakelins' interior decoration was derived from earth tones and the palette of natural materials – clay pamments, Portland stone, wide plank oak floors, lime plaster – and onto this were fused the natural dyes of hand-stitched Tibetan rugs and linens from Rogers and Goffigon. This was as close as imaginable to the experience of the Arts and Crafts architects – Charles Voysey, Edwin Lutyens, Mackay Hugh Baillie Scott – where all aspects of the house were drawn into a single vision.

The abstract architecture of the extension, a fractured cuboid broken along its spine into two slipped volumes – rear and front separated by a double-height void – was the first opportunity to date to create a non-referential architecture of sculptural abstraction. I felt at this point that I was beginning to understand for the first time what I had been trying inauthentically to do 20 years previously as a student. I had needed the siren voice of the past to seduce and detain me before I was ready to break away and discover a more personal expression. These ideas were further developed in a series of modern houses of varying scale over the following years to the present day, from the taut rural modesty of Glen View in Suffolk (see page 65) to the urbane reticence of Leaf House in London (see page 73) to the imperial spread of Fulford Farm in Northamptonshire (see page 31).

Houses

This was a turning point and from that moment on I became able to work and develop my own chosen style – always helped and influenced by those who collaborated with me. Over my

professional life as an architect, I have seldom ventured from the realm of the private house. I've remained preoccupied with the intricacies of the hearth: in so doing evading the challenges of the workplace and other typologies. I have found that the small scale of the domestic provides me with ample scope for formal expression despite the occasional conflicts that arise when my aspirations don't coincide with those of the client. While I should love to have deployed what skills I have in the public realm I remain relatively content to remain at home, so to speak, in the house.

Not that I feel residential architecture to be a support act. It is manifest that at many stages in the flux of theory and practice it is the house that has served as the medium and agent for radical change. At these trigger moments when culture lurches forward or sideways the house takes on an emblematic status beyond the contingencies of shelter and becomes a manifesto for how things might be, whether it be the escapism and romantic retrospection of William Burges and Baillie Scott or the embrace of modernism by Le Corbusier and the Bauhaus architects. Though few houses will exert the influence of the villas Savoye and Tugendhat or of the villas Capra and Pisani, the house continues to be an indulgent and permissive medium for formal and constructional experimentation. All this is possible given the preconditions of an enlightened planning regime, open-minded local politicians, enthusiastic and supportive patrons and an architect with something worth saying. Not much to ask.

The enduring fascination of the house lies in our intimate and tactile relationship with it – it is the theatre in which is played out our beginning, our ending and all the acts in between. It is the place we have to leave and lose and then must search for, perhaps quixotically, through our adult years. The house is physical, the home metaphysical. Clients are mistaken if they think it is in the gift of the architect to provide them with the latter. Our memories of childhood, the substance of our dreams, are inextricably linked to the houses we were raised in and during our adult life these

Above, left
The master bedroom in the new extension at Wakelins. An articulated ceiling of false beams and a fitted interior of French polished walnut. The bed confronts a large picture window that looks out to the rural landscape beyond.

Above
A study at Wakelins, panelled in oak with a Portland stone floor. The oak desk was designed for the room by James Gorst Architects.

Right
The north elevation of Wakelins overlooking the drive.

interiors and atmospheres return to beguile and haunt us with an almost searing intensity and sense of loss. In our dreams our lost families and homes are once again reassembled. It may well be that we have significant experiences in restaurants, libraries, underground car parks and football stadia, but only in the house, where the public mask is dropped, does the real action happen – this is the place where lives are wrecked and redeemed. The architect of the private house creates the *mise en scène* for these biographies. He cannot influence them – we are not emotional engineers. However, the spatial and formal properties of a house and the ways in which they are choreographed can create environmental atmospherics which can uplift or depress the human spirit. These atmospherics are generally not freshly determined *ab initio* by the architect but rather seep into the architect's work by osmosis and reflect the prevailing collective psyche of the culture at large. Only a few decades and Sigmund Freud separate Castle Drogo and Cragside from the villas Savoye and Tugendhat but the psychic distance between them is immense. From shuttered, panelled medievalism to the bright whiteness and transparency of the *plan libre* – from the castle to the sanatorium.

Introduction

As an architect and designer, one of the greatest strengths of James Gorst's work is an ability to craft spaces that seem simultaneously modern and timeless. Gorst's houses and interiors feel fresh, welcoming, practical and engaging, yet his buildings do not date overnight. They have depth, longevity and character – attributes that allow them to evolve, develop and change over time according to the needs of their owners and their families.

When it comes to house and home fashion can certainly be a dangerous thing. Constant shifts and changes in style and taste offer temptations to embrace trends that may be temporal so that, all too often, a 'contemporary' home can be left feeling dated and disjointed within the space of five or ten years. The notion of a 'timeless home' has, therefore, a positive allure particularly for those who would like to live beyond the here and now.

James Gorst is an architect who clearly takes the long view. His practice takes care to create plans and layouts that allow for a degree of flexibility and change. He steers away from fashion in favour of materials that have character and provenance, taking particular care over detailing and finish. His houses generally feature many bespoke elements – staircases, kitchens, seating, wardrobes and storage – that create a cohesive aesthetic while also providing clean and uncluttered spaces well suited to 21st-century living. At the same time Gorst's work is always highly contextual, forming a considered and careful response to both the needs of the client and the specific setting and surroundings.

As James Gorst eloquently explains in his foreword, the evolution of a design philosophy that is modern, contextual and 'timeless' is the result of his own personal journey through architecture and design. There are deep roots in both classicism and Arts and Crafts, with a rigorous approach to spatial planning and proportion combined with a love of fine, natural materials. Yet, as Gorst explains, he was determined to break away from these two models and adopt a third way that fuses lessons from both, spliced with the precepts and passions of modernism.

Over the last 20 years, following this third way, Gorst and his practice have established a reputation for homes in both town and country that are crafted and thoughtful. They combine modern thinking and an understanding of 21st-century patterns of living with an ingrained respect for craftsmanship and texture. There is a love for the heritage of the hearth, the kitchen and the library but also a passion for fluid homes that offer a journey from one space to another, with delights and surprises along the way. In many respects, Gorst's houses are the polar opposite of mass manufacture, providing tailored, layered and responsive homes.

Leaf House (see page 73) in north London, for example, garnered attention and praise because it managed to fuse past and present – or heritage and modernity – in one building. The outward form is linear and the family house is substantial in scale overall and this is also one of Gorst's more abstract and uncompromising compositions. Yet Leaf House draws on the familiar model provided by the period London townhouse, with the overall impact on the streetscape of this five-storey home respectfully reduced by a substantial basement level and a recessed third floor with a spacious study. There are bespoke elements throughout, including a crafted kitchen, a custom staircase and a delightful sense of connection between the key living spaces and the courtyard garden to the rear, which comes complete with a garden room. The overall plan is malleable enough to accommodate daily living and work, along with the shifting requirements of the family as the children grow older.

There are clearly common themes and threads – outlined above – that carry across Gorst's full portfolio. Yet each project is a new beginning, offering the opportunity to create afresh, and every challenge is a welcome catalyst. Even unbuilt projects (such as Roper's Farm in Essex, eventually turned down by the planners) have helped to progress new ideas, which are then developed and explored further in projects that follow on.

Despite occasional disappointments such as Roper's Farm, Gorst has been fortunate to work at very different scales and in contrasting contexts. These range from apartments in period buildings through to wholly new rural estates, which involve a collection of complementary structures and buildings. Gorst has always enjoyed shuttling between town and country, savouring the many pleasures and advantages offered by both. The practice has also worked to a range of budgets, ranging from high-specification luxury spaces through to the modest craftsmanship of country cabins such as Glen View (see page 65).

In general, whatever the budget, the practice has tended to involve itself in almost every aspect of a project including architecture, landscaping, interiors and furniture. This is not only an attractive proposition for clients but it results in projects that are cohesive and fully rounded, where the design narrative continues all the way through from start to finish. This, too, plays a part in creating spaces that feel complete and multi-layered. The projects over the following pages are intended to suggest the breadth and depth of the practice's work over two decades, ranging from rural estates through to urban pieds-à-terre. Each exemplar is, in its own special way, tailored and timeless.

Pages 22–23
Fulford Farm: the components of entry.

Opposite
The first floor entrance porch to the staff flat at Watergate.

Rural Estates

Rural Estates

The rural estates designed by James Gorst and his practice fuse influences and ideas drawn from a number of important traditions. These include the example of the traditional English country house, or country seat, but also the model of the vernacular farmstead where the farmhouse sits at the centre of a collection of complementary buildings, stables and agricultural sheds. Yet at the same time, Gorst's completed estates, with new residences of scale and substance at their heart, are also decidedly contemporary and draw on many principles and preoccupations laid down during the modernist period.

Gorst's Fulford Farm and Hannington Farm, both in Northamptonshire, can be placed within the grand tradition of the great English country house as it makes the transition into the 21st century. Placed carefully and considerately within the landscape, surrounded by hundreds of acres of farmland, these new family homes are buildings on an ambitious scale comparable with the great country houses of the past. They, too, sit within the context of working estates with farms, barns and outbuildings that form a rural collective.

Rather than seeking to impose themselves upon the countryside, as was so often the way with neoclassical country seats, Gorst's projects work with the land and its topography, seeking accommodation and understanding. Importantly, they seek a vivid and multifaceted relationship with the surroundings and a constant sense of connectivity. This is achieved not only through framed vistas and banks of glass, but also through courtyard spaces, walled gardens and terraces that create a hinterland between indoor and outdoor space.

Traditional farmsteads are another key source of inspiration, expressed within the architect's portfolio in a number of different ways. As with farmsteads, Gorst engages in a process of place-making, where a number of different buildings sit alongside one another, including barns and functional agricultural sheds. The houses themselves generally consist of a cluster of interconnected pavilions, often helping to cradle and protect an outdoor space in the manner of farm buildings around a farmyard. Many of Palladio's great Italian neoclassical houses were, of course, farmhouses on working estates and this synergy between the great house and the farm is never forgotten in Gorst's contemporary approach to the revival of an old typology in a new form.

Gorst's own relationship with the new rural estate goes back some years. Having designed and built a number of country houses (see following chapter), Gorst was asked to design a new home on an estate in West Sussex to serve, primarily, as a guest house to a larger house being built nearby in a neo-Jacobean style. Whithurst Lodge (see page 59) won a good deal of press attention, as well as a RIBA (Royal Institute of British Architects) award, which generated an enquiry in 2002 from a landowner near Chelmsford in Essex.

This potential client owned around 100 acres of farmland, known as Roper's Farm, not far from Writtle University College, with a small cottage and derelict farm buildings. He was hoping to build a new house on the site, plus a guest house, as well as restoring and reinstating barns and outbuildings. The resulting plan provided a new rural estate, with this collection of structures arranged around a large, open courtyard. Gorst's plans were well received by the client and supported by CABE (Chartered Association of Building Engineers), who described it in their 2003 Design Review Committee Recommendation as 'a well-considered and coherent building with a landscape design to match' adding that 'the relationship between the internal space and the landscape is drawing on the modern tradition, showing how modern thinking can add to the tradition of the country house'.

Pages 26–27
The entrance facade of Fulford Farm. An ironstone wall emerges from the turf and grows, as the land drops, to rise and culminate in the three-storey tower.

Importantly, the house was submitted to the local planning authority under a relatively new clause at that time known as Planning Policy Guideline 7 (PPG7, or the 'Gummer Clause', after the then environment minister John Gummer), which allowed for a one-off, new house in the countryside as long as 'it is clearly of the highest quality, is truly outstanding in terms of its architecture and landscape design, and would significantly enhance its immediate setting and wider surroundings'. Unfortunately for Gorst and his client, in the early days of PPG7 the clause was predominantly used to gain permission for neoclassical country homes, with very few modern designs making it through. Despite the enthusiastic endorsement of the local planning department with a recommendation for approval, the application for Roper's Farm was rejected on parochial political grounds by councillors keen to garner votes in the forthcoming elections.

It was a bitter pill for Gorst and his practice, who had invested a great deal of time, energy and imagination in the project. But it did provide a kind of prototype for a country house that was both grand and modern, that explored the idea of various wings and associated structures arranged around a courtyard, while also seeking a strong and sensitive relationship to the landscape.

'Roper's Farm was a very important step in developing our thinking about this kind of project', says Gorst. 'When you go through the design and planning process over six months or so, you are inhabiting the house as you design it. You are thinking about all of the volumes and spaces, as well as the different relationships between them, so in creating Roper's conceptually I had prepared myself for doing a house on a similar scale, which became Fulford.'

In 2004, PPG7 was replaced by Planning Policy Statement 7 (PPS7), which suggested that 'very occasionally the exceptional quality and innovative nature of the design of a proposed, isolated new house may provide this special justification for granting planning permission'. Furthermore, PPS7 stated that 'such a design should be truly outstanding and ground breaking' and that 'the value of such a building will be found in its reflection of the highest standards in contemporary architecture'.

This fresh emphasis, in PPS7, on innovation and contemporary architecture was vital for the progress of both Fulford and then Hannington Farm, both of which passed through the planning process under the clause (which has since been replaced by Paragraph 55 of the National Planning Policy Framework with a similar wording).

Both of these grand but contemporary country houses draw on certain ideas first developed at Roper's Farm, while forging a vital but respectful connection with the landscape. Each of these projects offers a kind of micro-village or community in miniature, with a series of farm buildings, while the 'big house' is broken down into a series of intersecting forms arranged around a courtyard. As well as the farm and the grand country house, the other key point of inspiration is the campus.

'The thing that I particularly loved when I was at Cambridge was going through the college gatehouse and then into the courtyard', says Gorst. 'That's a particular theme that runs through all of these projects, with this interplay of openness and enclosure. You come in and step out, but you are still protected. There is a delight in that idea.'

Fulford Farm

Northamptonshire
2004

Composed of a collection of farm buildings as well as a striking and substantial modern residence, this Northamptonshire home designed by James Gorst marks a significant renaissance in the idea of the English country estate. During the 1950s and 1960s, within an era of post-war austerity, many traditional English rural estates struggled and a number of fine period country houses were demolished after falling into dereliction. Heritage listing protected many others from the same experience, but the revival of the great estates has been a gradual process and the creation of new estates – anchored by a house of scale and architectural merit – is still a rarity.

Gorst suggests that Fulford Farm represents one of the first new English rural estates, designed as a single project, since the Edwardian era. Certainly, given its distinctly modern character (as opposed to 21st-century neoclassicism) it is exceptional and extraordinary in its sense of ambition, forming part of a 400-hectare property, devoted to arable farming but punctuated by woodland.

The project was commissioned by a private client, who bought the site complete with an undistinguished house dating from the 1980s. This set some precedent for the new residence, but planning permission was granted under Planning Policy Statement 7, which allows for one-off houses of 'exceptional quality'. As part of the project, Gorst designed a new farm, with barns, sheds and outbuildings to serve the estate, as well as to provide space for a biomass heating plant fed by woodchip.

The new country house sits at one remove from the farm, with its own driveway, which forms part of the processional approach. The house itself is on a large scale, at around 36,000 square feet, and has been arranged over two principal levels, with the addition of a more modest second storey space and also a basement level, which holds a private cinema and other family amenities. Local ironstone, with a reddish tinge, was used to clad the house, lending it a degree of monumentality in the landscape. Extensive glazing in certain parts of the building adds transparency and lightness which creates a vivid contrast to the mass implied by the stonework.

The plan is effectively a pinwheel, but with a good deal of complexity contained within its 'spokes', which revolve around the fulcrum of the main entrance and a soaring hallway. The house is composed of a series of linear stone pavilions, but of different heights, offering a staggered sequence of sculptural forms. One of these wings extends outwards to help shelter a courtyard garden facing southwards, contrasting with the open views of the landscape to the north.

Pages 30–31
From the pool house across the courtyard to the kitchen wing – like an ironstone pueblo.

Below
The ground-floor plan.

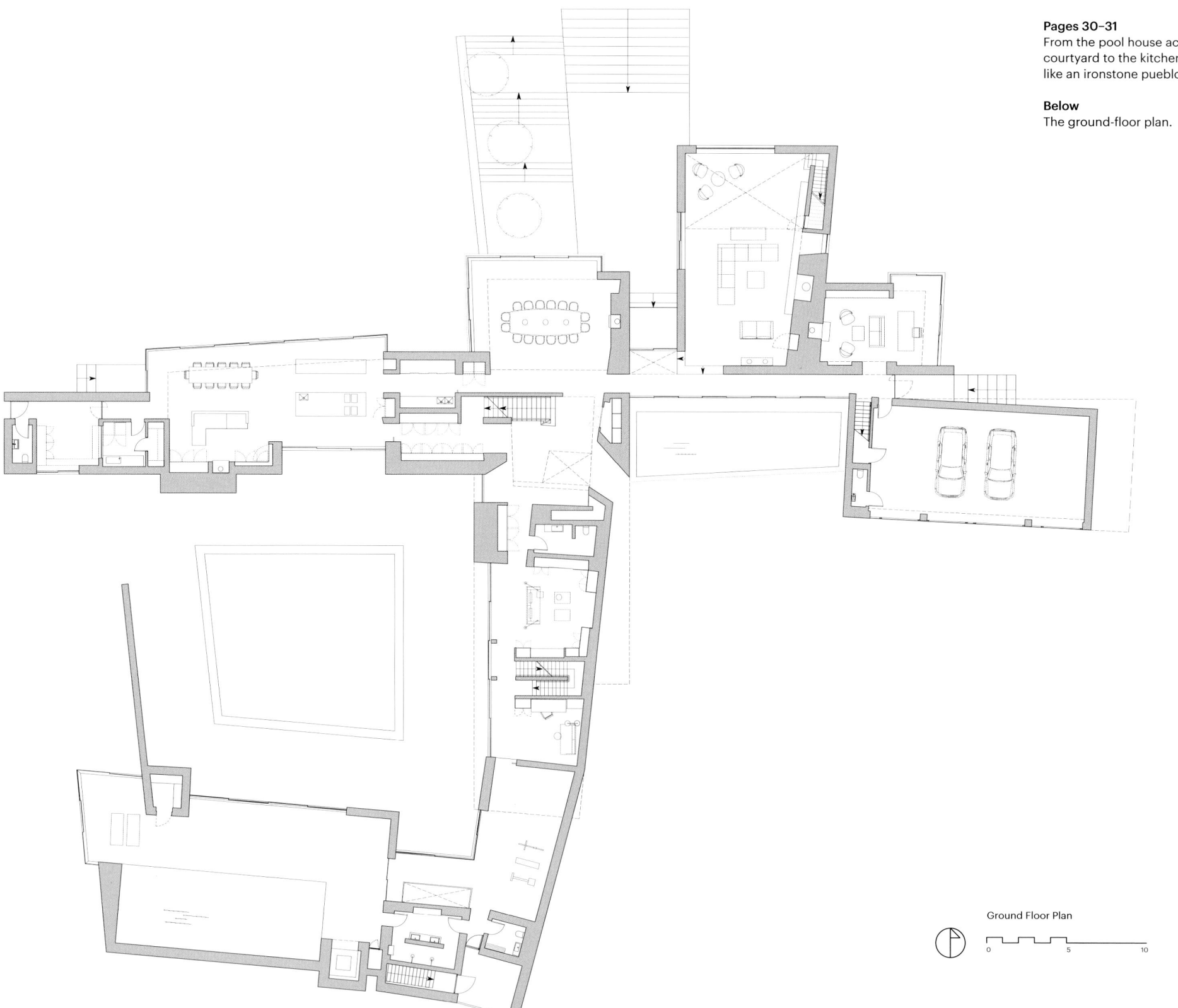

Ground Floor Plan

Above
A study.

Right
The mezzanine library enfolded in a wrap of polished Italian walnut.

'You could see the house as a series of buildings and the architectural journey through them is almost like travelling along through the streets of a small town and discovering courtyards, piazzas and other spaces', says Gorst. 'But you can only really achieve that because of the overall scale of the project. Normally, within a compact house, you have to create that journey, or promenade, in much more subtle ways. One of the reasons that I love courtyards especially is that you can look across them and see another part of the same house and whatever might be happening in that space. It's a very special feeling of being enclosed and connected at one and the same time.'

A reflecting pool sits close to the entrance, helping to frame the approach but also adding a calm, soothing and natural note that reinforces the notion of welcome. The angled front door leads into an open atrium, top-lit, with stone floors and walnut wall panelling, reminiscent of Arts and Crafts country houses by Edwin Lutyens and Charles Voysey, although the treatment here is contemporary. Secret cupboards set flush into the panelling offer functional storage solutions while the materials are expressive, organic and warm.

Each spoke of the pinwheel, arranged around the axis of the entry hallway, serves a purpose. The main sitting room complete with a focal point hearth sits in one wing with a private study to one side and the timber-panelled formal dining room nearby. Another spoke has been devoted to a large open-plan kitchen combined with a casual dining area and family lounge space, collectively offering a framed panorama of the open countryside.

The journey of discovery continues around the courtyard until one reaches the swimming pool, featuring a wall of Cumbrian slate to one side, with natural light washing in from a long skylight above. A seating area beside the pool looks across the courtyard, while there is also a gym close by. Shifts in proportion, volume and light help to differentiate one space from another during the journey through the home.

'What I try to do in all of my houses is create this unfolding sequence of different and varied spatial experiences, as well as offering vistas and sight lines that connect one space to another', says Gorst. 'So you are never stuck in one room or come to a dead end – there is always this sense of opening out and coming across something new.'

Including the tower bedroom on the uppermost level, there are six bedrooms arranged across the house, with specific areas devoted to children, guests and the master suite. There are additional surprises, such as the panelled library floating on a mezzanine level above the main sitting room, as well as the luxuries of the basement, including the cinema and billiard room.

Importantly for a contemporary country house, the connections back to the landscape are constant and engaging, with key views framed and articulated with care from the double-height window in the sitting room, through to the 'treetop' vantage point from the tower. The open land becomes a key pleasure in itself, appreciated from all parts of the residence, constantly shifting and changing according to the seasons.

Below
The entrance to the house. The external shelter of the cantilevered outcrop, the un-fenestrated stone walls, the robust bronze doors and reflecting pool are reminiscent of a medieval castle and the narrative of arrival, entry and refuge.

Right
The triple-height entrance hall. Austere like a Wren church with stone floor, white plaster and dark wood.

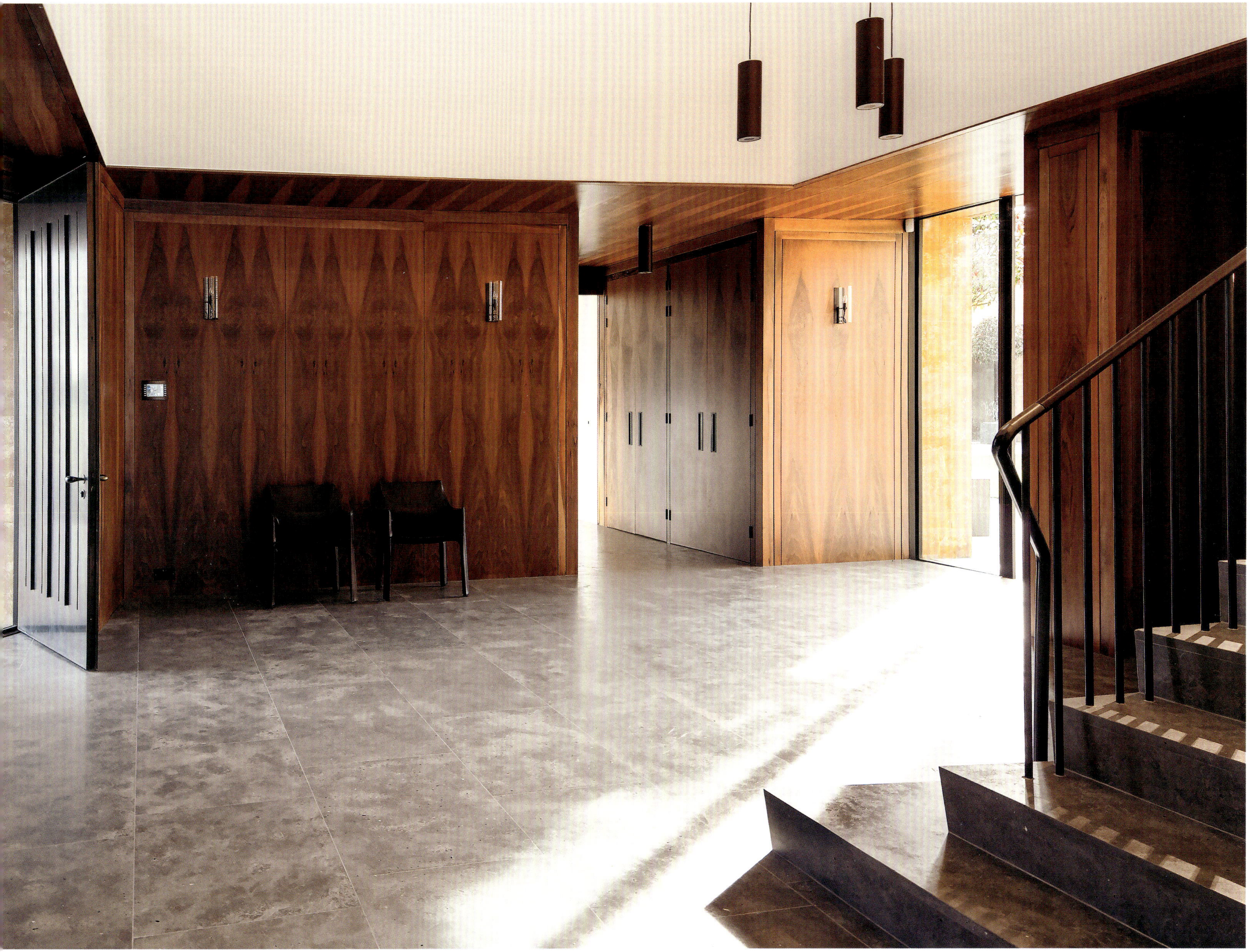

Above
The decumanus – the long east–west corridor from garage to kitchen.

Opposite
The 'mannerist' entrance with its oversailing stone box resting on a fragile glass screen.

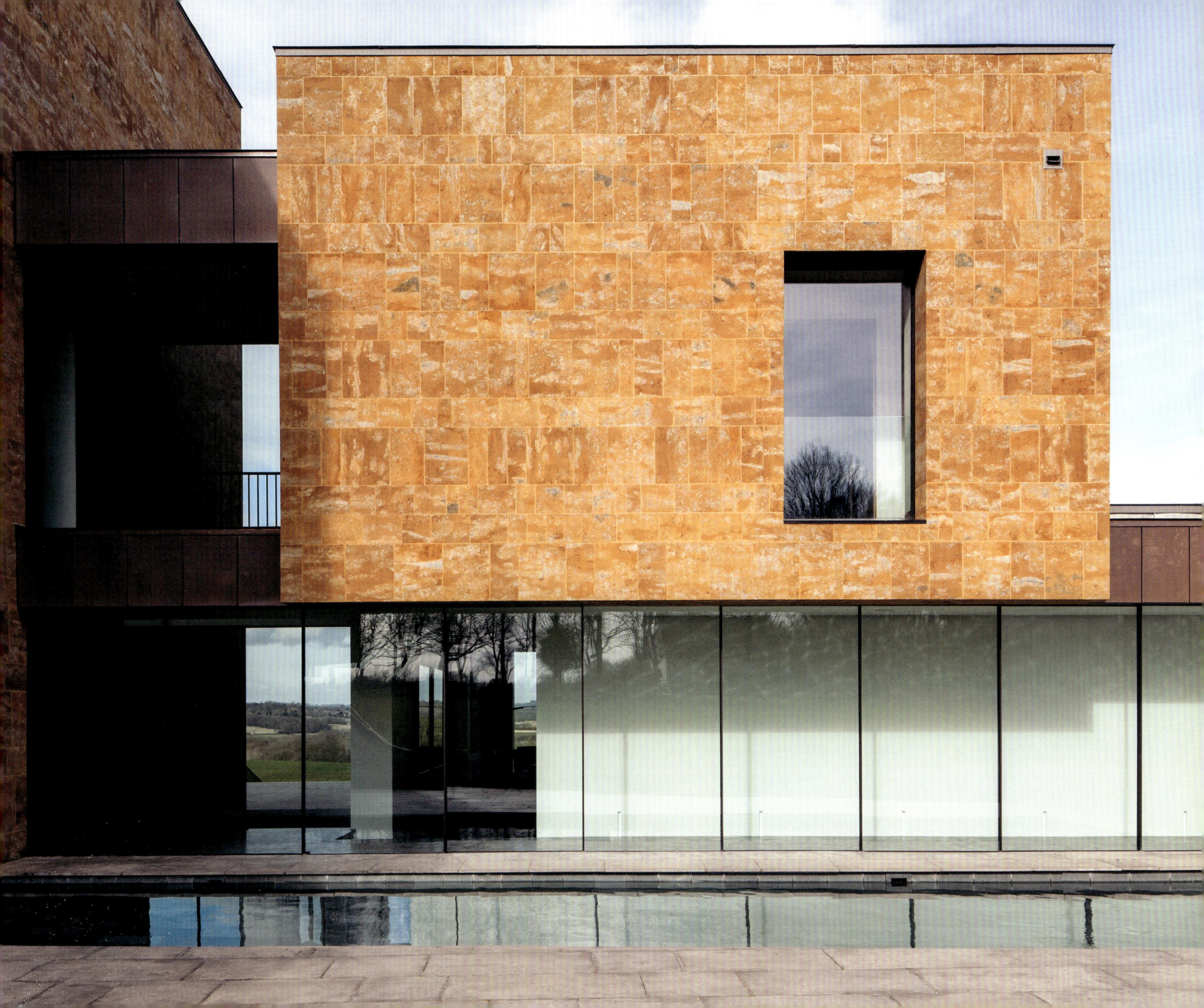

Left
Consummate ashlar stonework: the elision of two planes creating a small point of visual interest.

Rural Estates: Fulford Farm

Above
Bronze and Banbury blue ironstone on a winter's day.

Above
The north elevation with its sweeping steps leading up to the fulcrum where the spokes of the house meet and conjoin.

Rural Estates: Fulford Farm

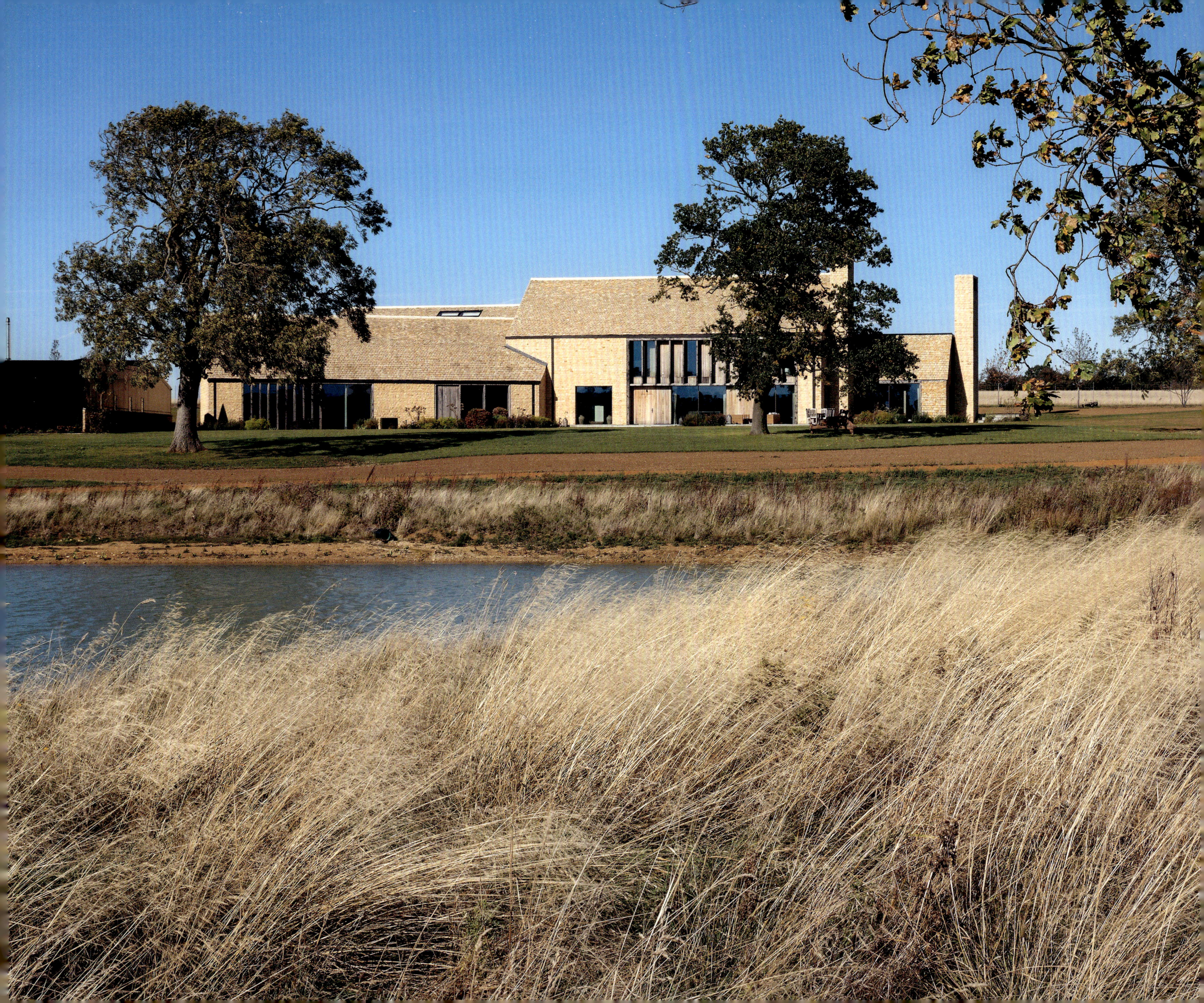

Hannington Farm

Northamptonshire
2016

Traditional farmsteads provide comfortable synergy with the surrounding landscape. They sit naturally within the topography, seeking shelter, rather than imposing themselves upon the land. They are, in themselves, formed from a cluster of buildings, barns and sheds of which the farmhouse itself becomes the hub and heart. Yards and other sheltered spaces in between serve as 'rooms' in themselves, with a true sense of purpose, while materials tend to be locally sourced and in keeping with vernacular traditions. All of these characteristics and more are central to the essential charm of the farmstead.

James Gorst's Hannington Farm, set within 300 acres of Northamptonshire farmland, draws on many of these conventions yet is also distinctly contemporary in character. This new farmstead is, indeed, a cluster of complementary structures placed in the landscape in a thoughtful, considered manner. The cladding is made of locally sourced stone (Cotswold limestone) and extensive use is made of timber. Yet in its outline, spatial and volumetric planning, as well as in its level of sophistication and detailing, Hannington is very much a 21st-century home.

The family house was commissioned by clients who had acquired the acreage, along with derelict red brick farm buildings. They wanted to build a new home to a high standard and specification, while restoring the landscape and establishing a deer park and shoot with an emphasis on sustainability and respect for the natural environment. At the same time, there was also a need for children's spaces and room for guests.

Gorst began by looking at the placement of the new buildings in the landscape, including the new residence and a separate barn nearby with stables and facilities, as well as storage for the deer farm. The new buildings were placed not far from the former farmstead but set within a natural fold in the landscape.

'The contours of the land helped to generate the early ideas for the scheme', says Gorst. 'We decided to create two artificial lakes, fed by a stream, below the house, which also receive all the rainwater from the buildings. Because the house sits within this fold, you don't see the house as you approach until quite late in the journey and then you reach the barn on a crest and begin to drop down to the house itself.'

This gradual process of discovery connects with a thoughtful *promenade architecturale* as one approaches the two- to three-storey farmhouse itself, with a V-shaped entry courtyard leading towards the front door. As with Fulford, the overall plan is, more or less, a pinwheel with three distinct

Pages 42–43
Hannington Farm, looking to the north across the newly landscaped lake.

Left
The side elevation of the house, offering vivid contrasts between mass and transparency.

Opposite
From a distance, the towering crafted chimneys are reminiscent of the high towers of a Tuscan hill town.

Rural Estates: Hannington Farm

wings revolving around a triple-height entrance hall with the stairwell alongside. From the outside, the three wings read as an interlinked cluster of structures, each with a pitched roof, but with variations in height and orientation that lend character to the house as a whole. The entire building is clad in stone with stone shingles for the roofs, creating a pleasing sense of cohesion and unity. Three tall stone chimneys tower upwards, forming strong vertical lines in the landscape and contrasting with the diagonals of the pitched roofs.

'All of the pitched roofs are asymmetrical, so it looks reassuring but it is about taking the vernacular and giving it a twist', says Gorst. 'The chimneys are almost like Italianate campaniles and we are very pleased with those – you could say that it's almost like San Gimignano in the Northamptonshire countryside.'

Within, the three wings are dedicated to specific functions and uses, with a number of significant shifts in volume and proportion. The main living spaces are housed within the most complex part of the house spatially, with an open-plan kitchen connecting with a dining area alongside and then onwards to a double-height drawing room; here the sense of volume is striking and barn-like in itself, while the cross-laminated timber beams that support the roof are left exposed and offer a sculptural presence in the space. The master suite sits on the first floor in this part of the building, with an additional bedroom on a modest second floor.

Below left
From the entrance hall to the drawing room.

Below
From the kitchen to the wine store.

Opposite
The endoskeletal drawing room.

Rural Estates: Hannington Farm

Left
The swimming pool.

Above right and left
The master bedroom and bathroom with the galleried study above.

Of the other two wings, one is dominated by a double-height indoor swimming pool. Again, the sense of scale and volume is striking, with the exposed stone walls contrasting with the black ceramic tiles used to line the pool itself. A gym and other facilities sit alongside, plus a charcuterie and wine cellar; an additional bedroom and service spaces above are accessed by a secondary staircase.

The third and final wing offers a mix of functional spaces on the ground floor – including a boot room and storage spaces – plus a family room and a games room. Three children's bedrooms sit on the floor above, which include mezzanine sleeping platforms up in the eaves. The tripartite plan of the house not only allows for specific functions at ground floor level, but also gives parents, children and guests their own semi-private zones on the upper floors. Detailing and execution is to the highest standard, with bespoke elements throughout, including the crafted staircase with its walnut banister and oak treads.

Yet Hannington never forgets that it is a farmhouse on a working farmstead. As well as the charcuterie and gun room, there are bespoke kennels with heated floors, as well as other functional, agricultural spaces within the barn complex nearby.

'The clients were really passionate about getting the house built to create this unique place for their children to grow up in', says Gorst. 'They were very keen to create a family home that would be there for the duration and we wanted to carry the design process through to every detail, so that you get this seamless connection between the architecture and the interiors. It's not just about creating a shelter but about completing the whole picture.'

Echoing, once again, traditional farmsteads, Hannington offers contrasts between open, family spaces and more private retreats, such as the mezzanines, which are reminiscent of attic spaces in period country houses. Importantly, the level of craftsmanship also offers texture and warmth, adding to the intrinsic character of this very modern farm.

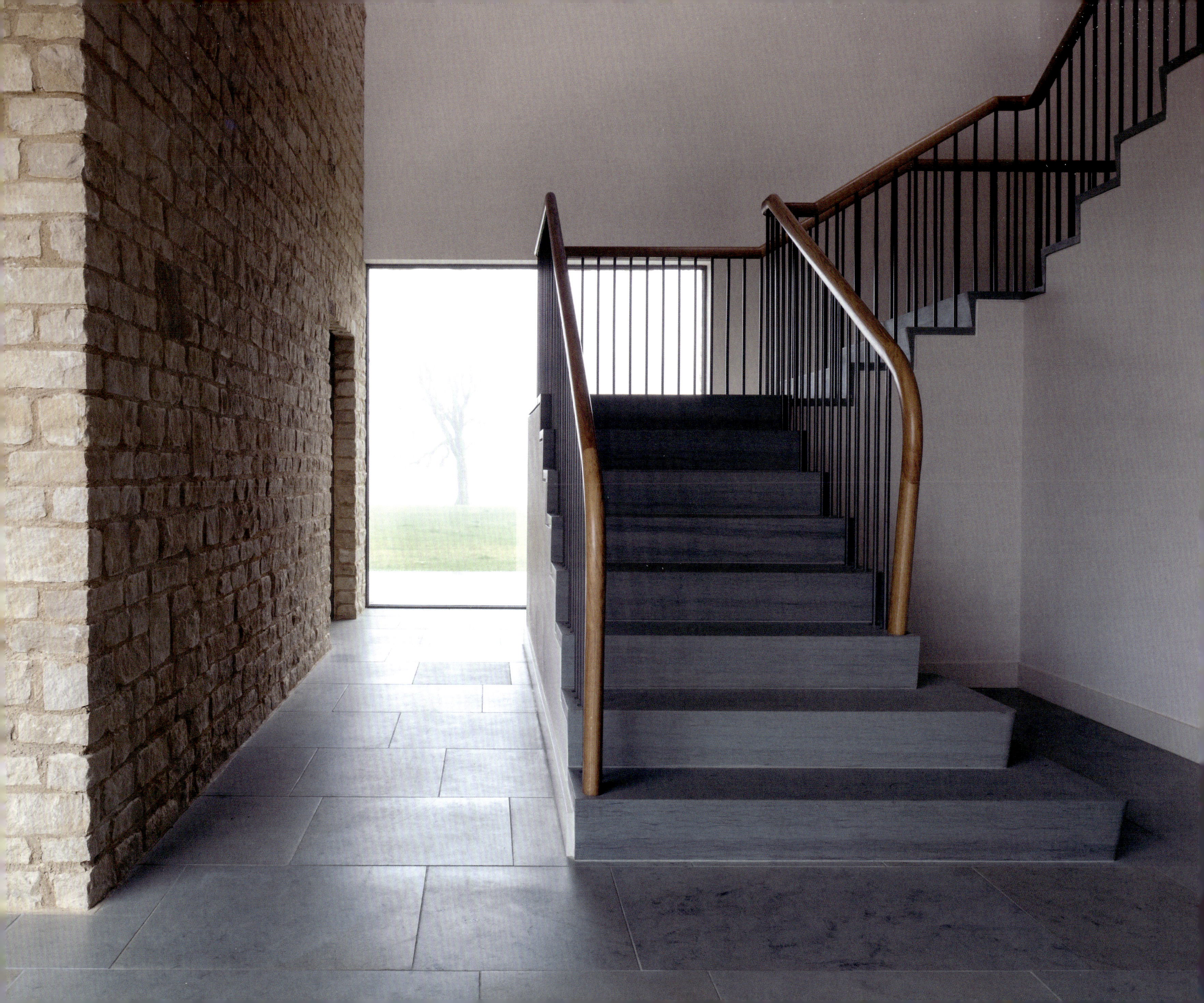

Opposite
The main stair with a view of landscape beyond, the kitchen wing to the left.

Right
The triple height staircase hall.

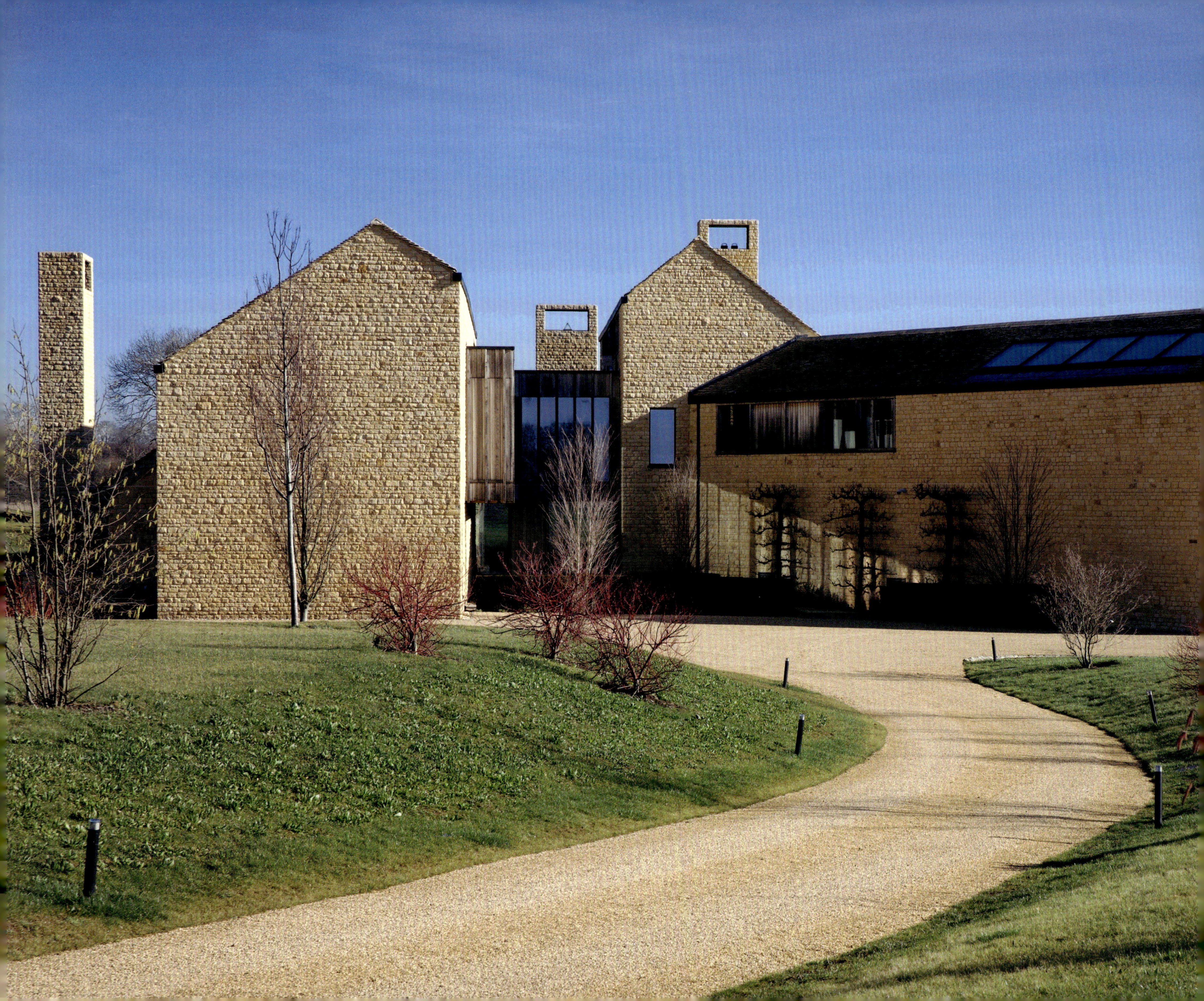

Right
The ground and first floor plans. The cranked axis of the plan follows the contours of the site. The drama of entrance is heightened by the projecting unfenestrated splayed wings that frame the recessed front door.

Left
The splayed wings draw the visitor deep into the heart of the building before entering.

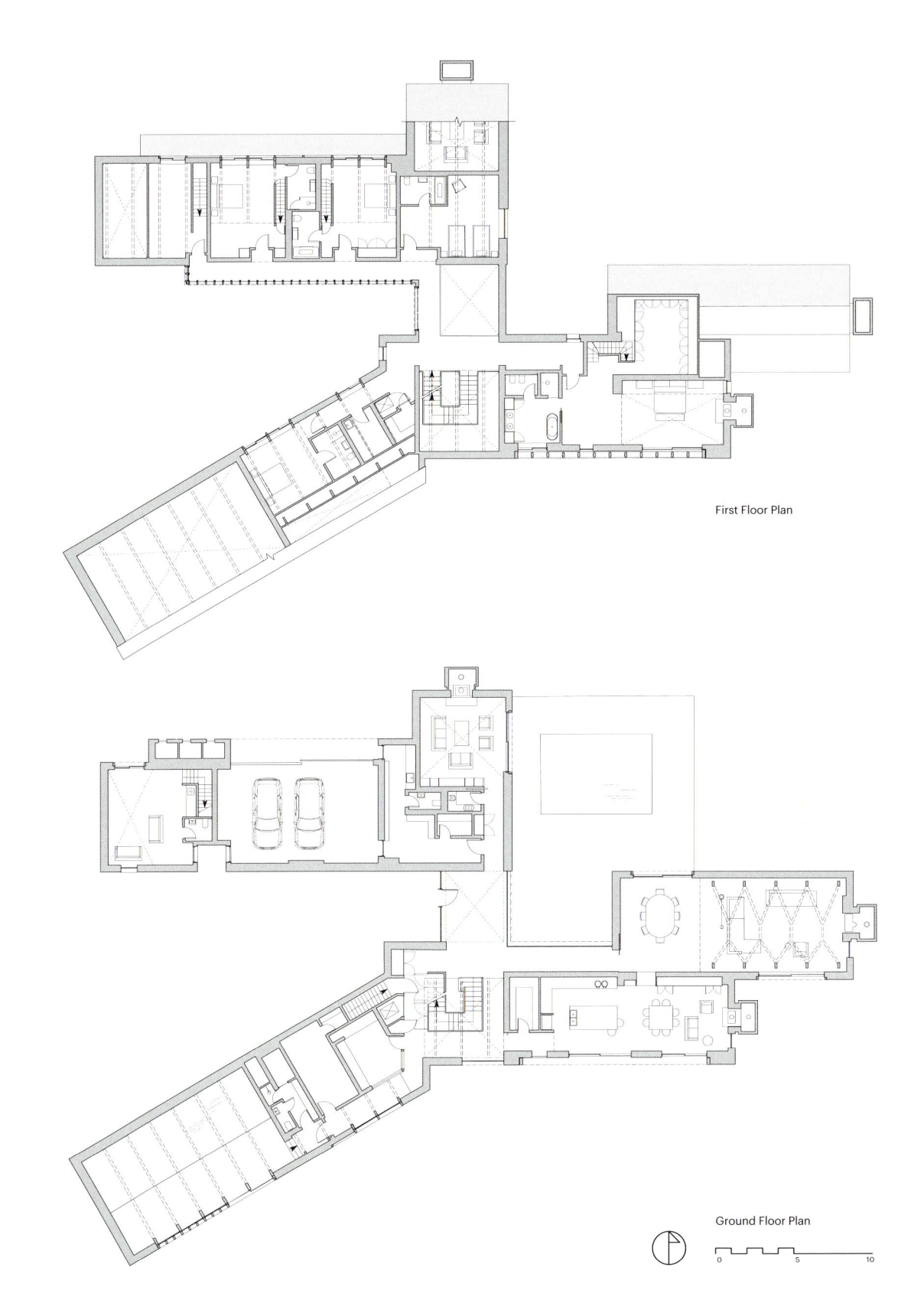

First Floor Plan

Ground Floor Plan

Houses

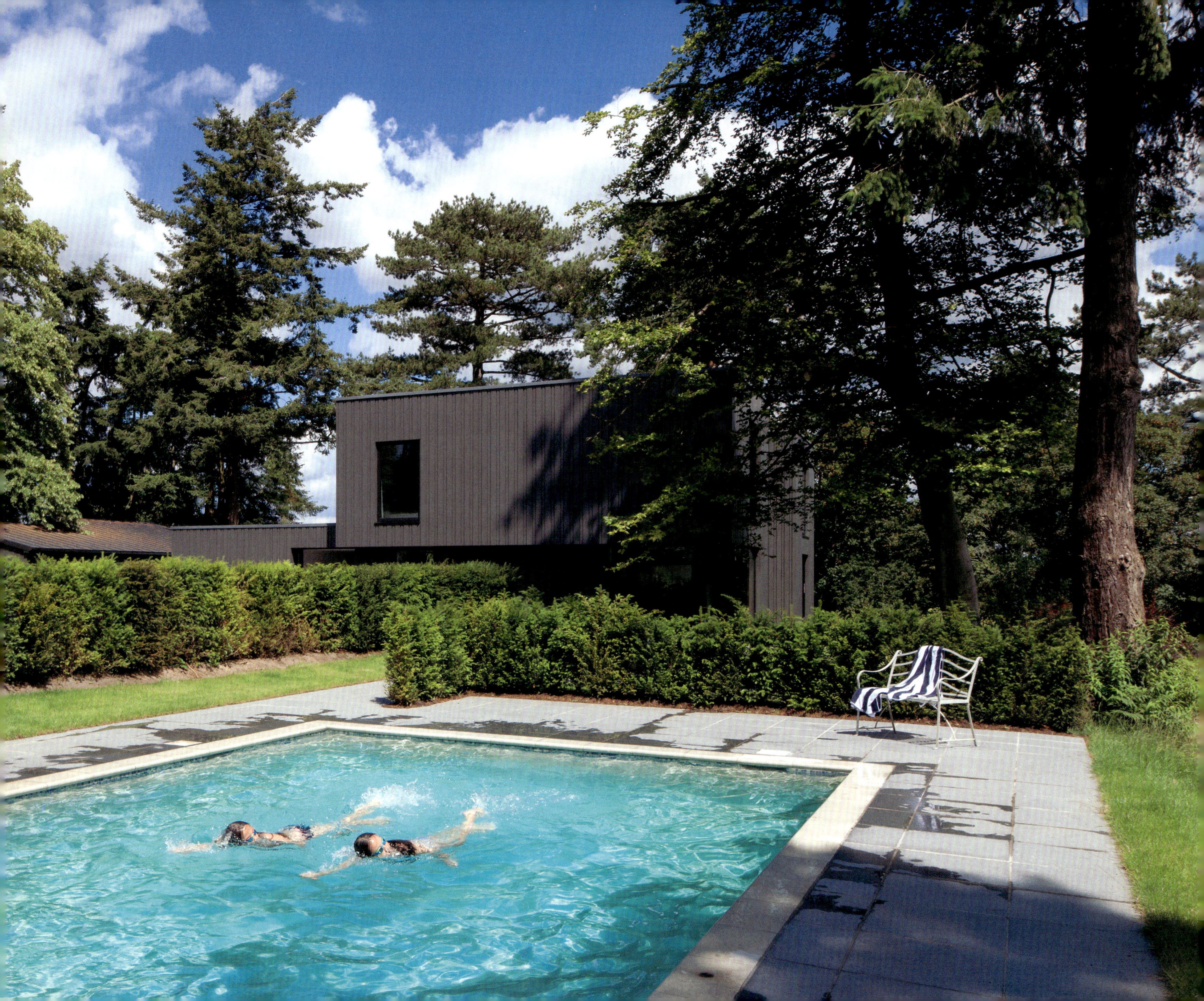

Pages 54–55
Sandpipers in Surrey.

Houses

While each and every one of James Gorst's houses is founded upon a set of solid architectural principles – with foundations derived from both classicism and modernism – there is also a degree of subversion within his work. As well as being functional and practical, Gorst takes great care to provide character and individuality, which comes – in part – from an imaginative approach to form. Stepping away from everyday solutions and experimenting with typologies gives Gorst the opportunity to create country houses, cabins and urban retreats infused with a sense of originality.

'Insofar as it's possible – given the demands of the clients and the restrictions of working within the relatively small scale of residential architecture – I am always looking to extract sculptural potential in relation to form', says Gorst. 'So, in some ways, I am looking to exceed the brief and perhaps design something that doesn't look like a conventional house. It's about subverting expectations in one way or another.'

A degree of positive subversion, with a touch of playfulness, only becomes possible because there is a very serious and rigorous discipline at work as well. The sense of order that pervades all of Gorst's work, including his country houses, is always apparent, with great thought given to the way that spaces will work and function, as well as to essentials such as proportion and scale. The same is true of the way that living spaces connect with one another, with a particular focus on creating relationships between rooms that flow naturally from one to the next without any need for corridors. Such enfilades are relatively informal but add to the gradual process of discovery that is so important to Gorst's design philosophy.

One of Gorst's earliest country houses was Pie Corner in Hertfordshire (1990, see pages 11–12). This house sits in an open rural setting, allowing the highly symmetrical form of the building to shine out. The house can be seen as a fusion of a pared down neoclassical villa, upon a compact footprint, with the work of Swiss architect Mario Botta, whose early rural and mountain houses were a source of inspiration for Gorst. With their strong, uncompromising sculptural outlines in concrete, brick or stone, Botta's early buildings often incorporated subversions of geometrical forms, such as indented terraces or inset apertures of one kind or another, often at irregular intervals.

Pie Corner is relatively pure in its symmetry, while the internal plan 'was driven by the formal symmetries of the geometry with no regard for the functional claims of competing domestic activities and yet seemed to work very well as a house for a family with four young children', as Gorst puts it. The modernity of the house was subtly expressed in the way that the spaces flowed and sang, along with the questioning of neoclassical conventions that help to lend this house of brick a degree of abstraction and individuality.

Later, as Gorst's began to step away from classicism, the houses assumed a more contemporary dynamic and a significant degree of abstraction. Symmetry was increasingly explored in more contemporary ways and often challenged, but the focus on order remained, with the rigour of the design process ensuring that the practice's houses work so well for modern living. This applies all the way through the house, from the floor plan to the detailing of practical elements, such as an ergonomic kitchen or integrated storage in key parts of Gorst's highly tailored homes.

Context is another essential consideration among Gorst's country houses, as well as his urban projects. The houses on the following pages are a considered response to their setting and surroundings, providing a powerful sense of connection with the landscape. This is explored through inside-outside spaces such as terraces and verandas, as well as carefully framed vistas of the countryside.

More than this, Gorst takes vernacular references into account. At Whithurst Lodge, in West Sussex, the pure and endearing outline of the barn is one source of inspiration. At Glen View in Suffolk, the agricultural barn is – similarly – a point of reference, particularly the pitch-painted agricultural sheds and fishermen's huts of the region. So, too, is the notion of the cabin with its combination of organic materials and conservative scale.

In many respects, Whithurst and Glen View offer a thematic pair, sharing some common characteristics, even if the resulting buildings are highly individual. The same can be said of Sandpipers in Surrey and the Brick House in Aldeburgh, Suffolk. Here, the focus is more on the 'exploration of a domestic architecture of sculptural forms and intense materiality', expressed in two linear houses clad in timber (Sandpipers) and brick. In both buildings, the precision of the geometry has been challenged and subverted, yet the materiality of each lends them a very different character.

The two projects underline how important the curation of materials has become throughout Gorst's work as a whole, outside and in. They are an intrinsic part of each house, chosen for their texture, provenance and individuality, whether that might be a locally sourced, handmade brick or sustainably sourced timber cladding or oak joinery for the interiors. For country houses, especially, the palette tends to be organic and natural, as well as practical and functional, while the craftsmanship involved in the successful assimilation of such materials is also a vital component.

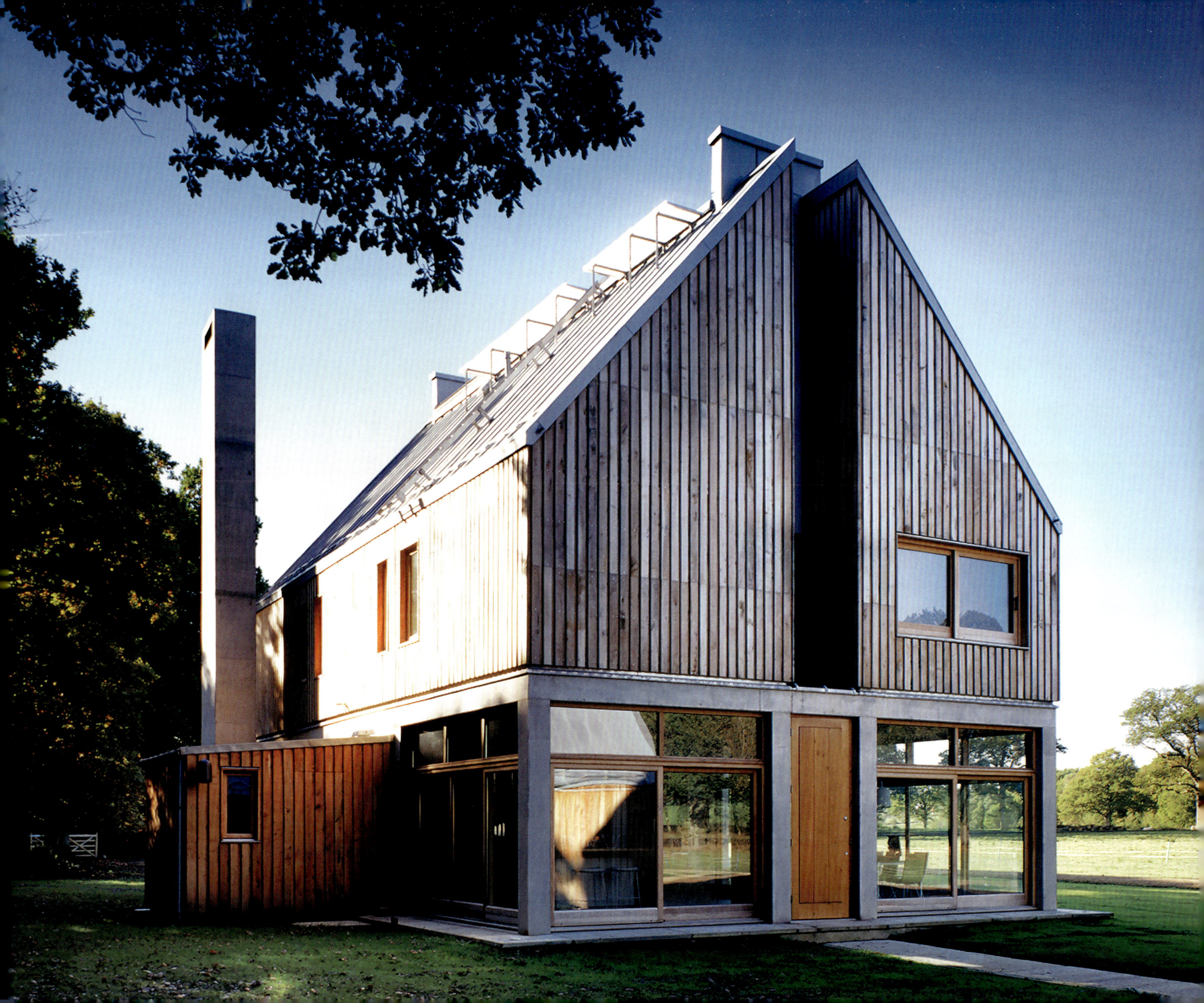

Whithurst Lodge

West Sussex
2001

Buildings that sit in an open landscape have a particular power and presence. They become sculptural forms framed by nature, but also floating in space, like a temple, a folly or a work of land art. With Whithurst Lodge in West Sussex, James Gorst was presented with a site open to a meadow, which forms part of a larger country estate. But rather than positioning the house in the open, Gorst decided to push the house towards the tree line, offering a backdrop of woodland with views out across the grassland.

'I had just been on a trip to Finland before designing the Lodge and I noticed, while I was on the train going through the countryside hour after hour, that all of the houses tend to be built up against the woods with an open pasture in front', says Gorst. 'I liked that contrast, with this slightly fearsome and unknown world of the forest and then the world of reason and light that is the meadow. I also wanted to feed that into the house itself, so that the ground floor is open to the landscape but the top floor is much more enclosed, cased in wood, like the forest and so it becomes a place of dreams.'

The canopy of the trees behind still allows the form of the house to stand out, offering a vivid green canvas. Gorst took a degree of inspiration from the vernacular form of the barn, reinforced by the use of locally sourced oak for the cladding on the upper level, as well as the introduction of an echo provided by a smaller structure alongside, providing garaging and storage. This smaller piece together with the Lodge – offering a mother and child composition – offers a farmstead in miniature.

'Barns are very pure structures', says Gorst. 'I suppose that purity and simplicity appeals to architects. It's a unified thing, without extensions, and a very clear architectural solution. But when you set up a repetitive, formal gridded structure – like Whithurst – then it's good to also subvert it, otherwise you can end up with something rather dull. Louis Kahn was the great exponent of this – setting up a formal arrangement and then denying it in some way.'

Here, Gorst plays with the exterior purity of a barn-style structure in a number of ways. To the front, the middle bay of the concrete-framed house is indented on the ground floor to create a kind of veranda. Upstairs, windows are placed at irregular intervals within the timber cladding. The entire house, including the zinc roof, is effectively split in two by an incision that includes a long skylight feeding down upon the central stairwell and spilling light deep into the building. A small outrigger to the rear, holding services, also erodes the linear, gridded format.

Inside the house the central staircase helps to define and order the spaces within. The interconnected dining area, study and seating area sit in three corners of the home, with the seating area focused upon a fireplace. The fourth corner holds the kitchen, a more enclosed pantry and then additional services in the outrigger.

On the upper level the plan also revolves around the stairwell, with internal windows looking out and over it, offering an inversion of the ground floor layout. There are three bedrooms plus the bathrooms. The master bedroom includes a 'door to nowhere' – an aperture that frames a view of the meadow and introduces fresh air. The stairwell also aids natural ventilation, with an operable skylight that vents warm, stale air in the summer months.

For the interiors, locally sourced oak is also used extensively for the joinery – including the ceilings – and integrated elements such as storage cupboards, contrasting with the practical polished concrete floors used on the ground floor. The kitchen is fully bespoke, featuring a long breakfast bar that doubles as a worktop.

Whithurst won an RIBA Award, with the jury noting the combination of craftsmanship, quality and practicality. 'The building has integrity, consistency and conviction and could provide a beneficial inspiration to mass builders working in the region', said the RIBA committee's citation. In this way, Whithurst – like Glen View (see page 65) – can be seen as a kind of exemplar or prototype for a fresh approach to building new rural homes of character and delight.

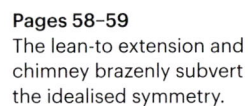

Pages 58–59
The lean-to extension and chimney brazenly subvert the idealised symmetry.

Right
The axial stair leading to the principal bedroom.

Above
Dining in the landscape.

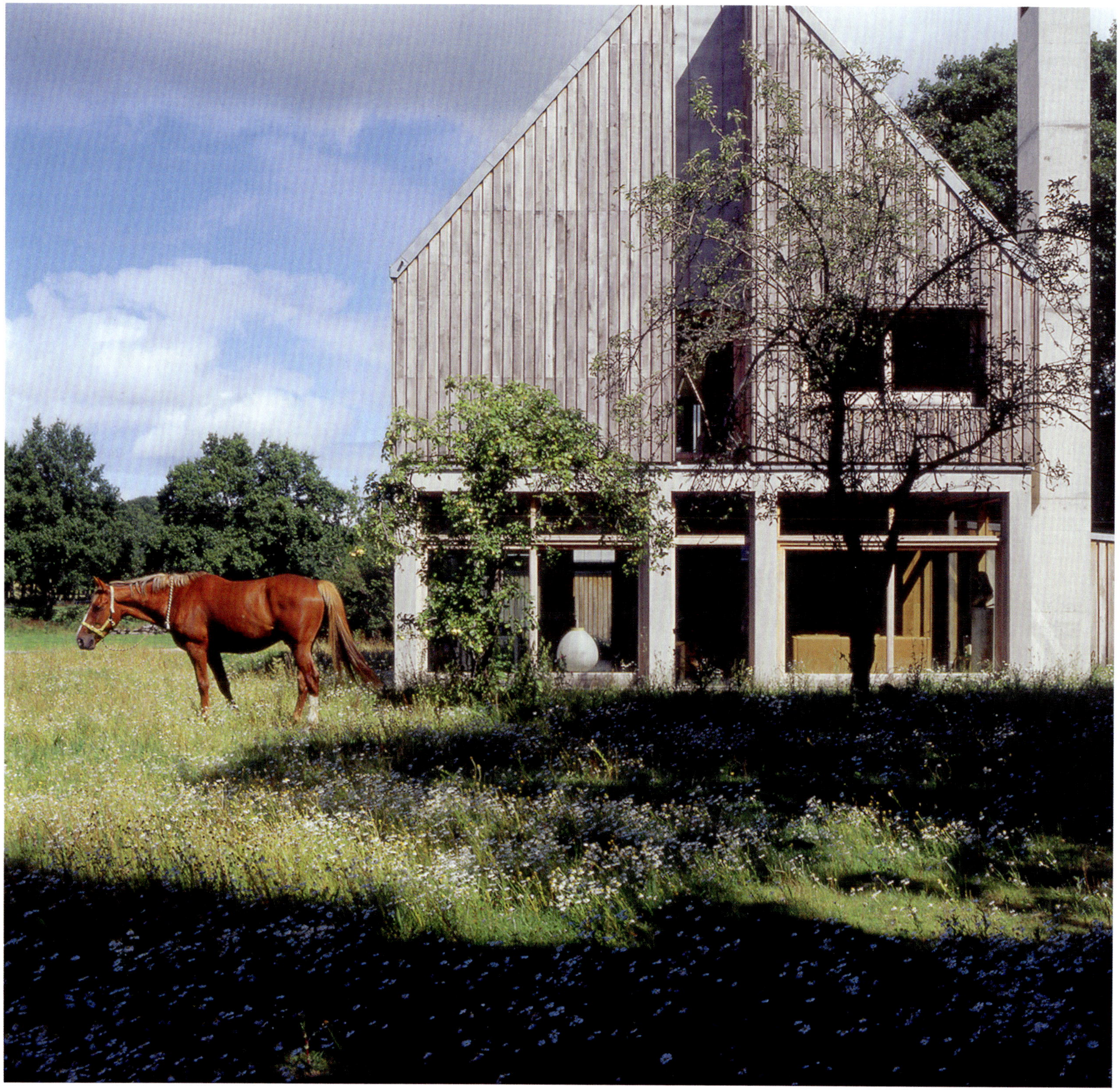

Below
The ground-floor plan.

Opposite
Spectral tones of silver and grey – oak, concrete, zinc – and a chestnut mare.

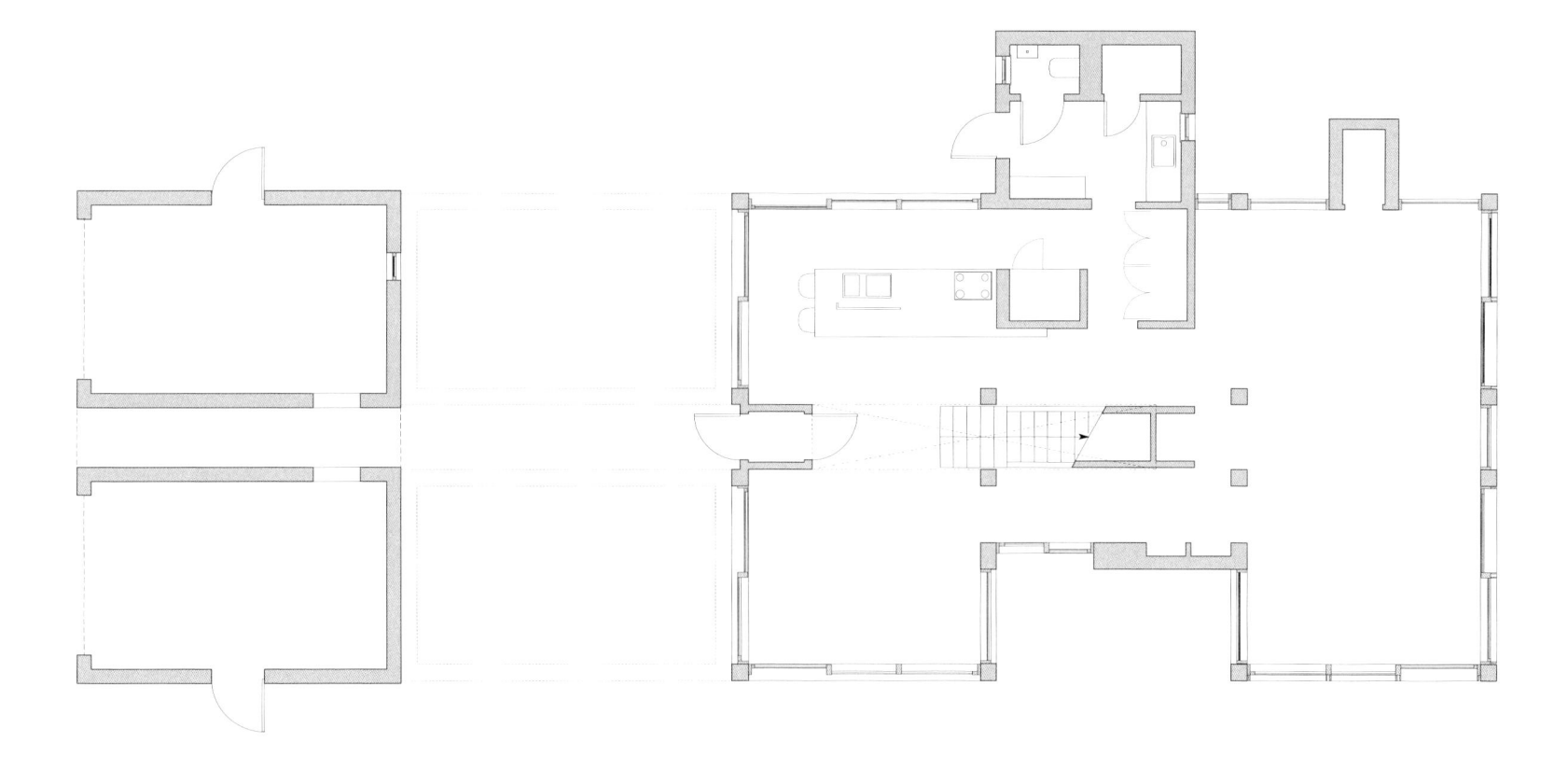

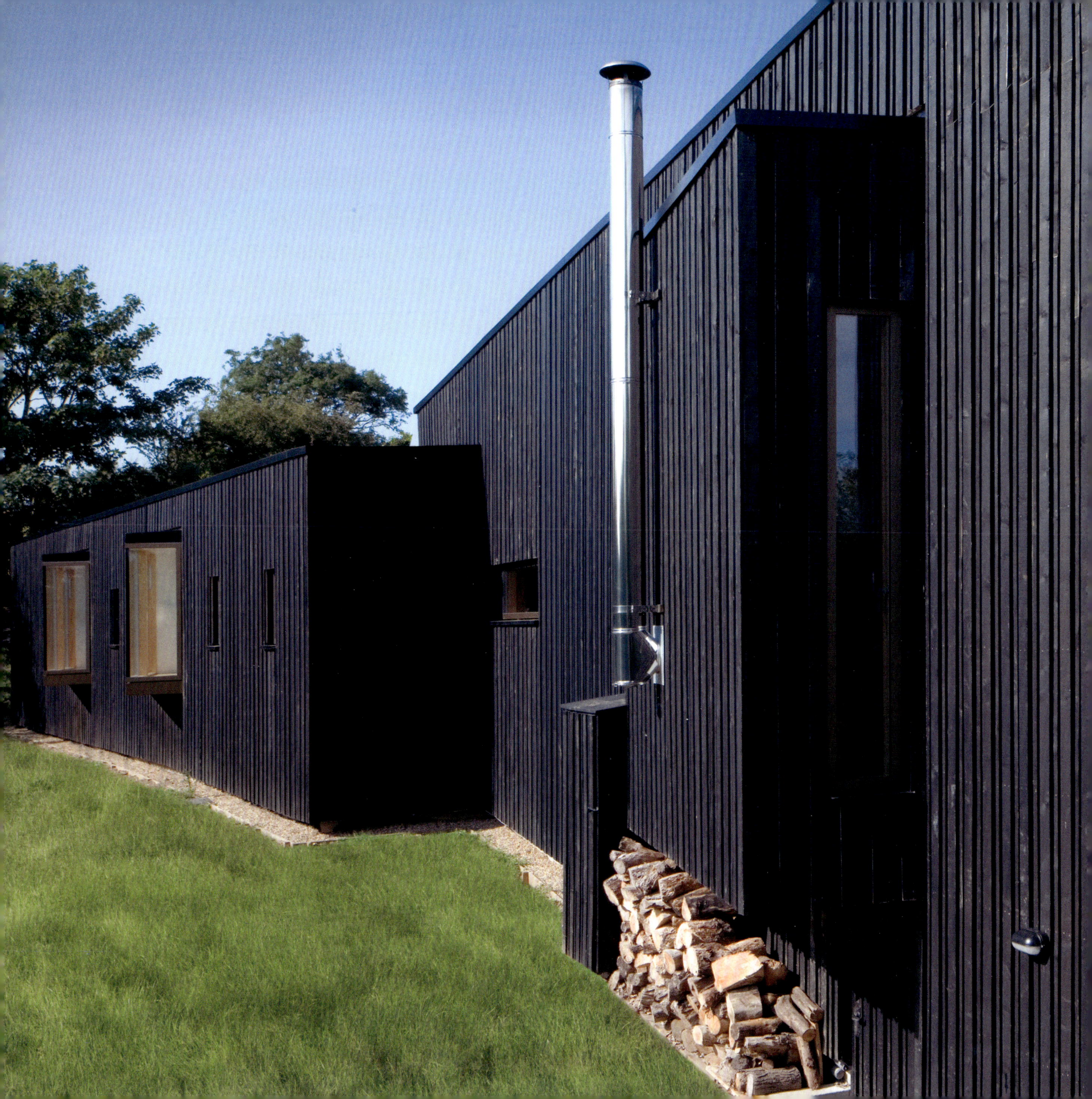

Glen View

Suffolk
2006

Sitting at the heart of a gentle and picturesque landscape, Glen View looks out upon open fields and mature trees. The single-storey house, tucked into the undulating topography, is subtle in its design and discreet, with its treated larch cladding reminiscent of East Anglian barns and agricultural buildings. Looking more closely, one sees a more contemporary silhouette, accentuated by the black pitch on the timber coat. There is also a conscious Scandinavian influence playing upon this modern cabin, with its modesty of scale combined with a crafted, modern aesthetic.

'I was quite inspired by the late work of the Swedish modernist architect Gunnar Asplund', says Gorst. 'He did some simple bungalows towards the end of his life, which are certainly very modest but also beautiful, with lovely moments and slight shifts and changes in the form and plan. Where you have these geometric shifts, then it signifies an important moment. But there's also a more general sensibility with Glen View towards materials that are quite Scandinavian – there's no frippery or excess.'

The house was designed for a private client as a rural retreat, replacing an existing bungalow on the site that dated from the 1930s. The budget for the build was relatively modest at just under £250,000, requiring a degree of imagination in order to achieve as much as possible within limited means. As such the project became a kind of prototype, in Gorst's mind, for a new generation of modern country houses that would be relatively affordable but also contextual and crafted.

Gorst used a prefabricated timber frame to help reduce cost and save time on site, with the building pushed lengthways into the slope of the hill. The principal living spaces were placed at the lower gradient (with high ceilings) and three bedrooms towards the rear (offering a more intimate scale). Sustainability was another key factor, working in synergy with the need to control costs. This applied not only to materials and staples – such as high standards and glazing to control heat loss and regulate temperatures within – but also to energy use as a whole.

Heating is provided by a ground-source heat pump, fed by a coil pipework system buried in the garden. This introduces warm water for the underfloor heating inside the house, with additional heat from a wood-burning stove. Glen View also draws water from its own dedicated well. Taking into account the sustainable sourcing of the materials – including elements such as reclaimed slate flooring – the carbon footprint of the house is minimal.

Within, the approach to the spatial dynamic of the building is also inventive. One steps into a semi-sheltered hallway, partially

The Timeless Home

Pages 64–65
The junction of the bedroom wing and the main living space.

Left
A large asymmetrically placed window observes life passing along the lane nearby.

Opposite
Glen View from the cornfield. An unobtrusive house that rises as the land drops.

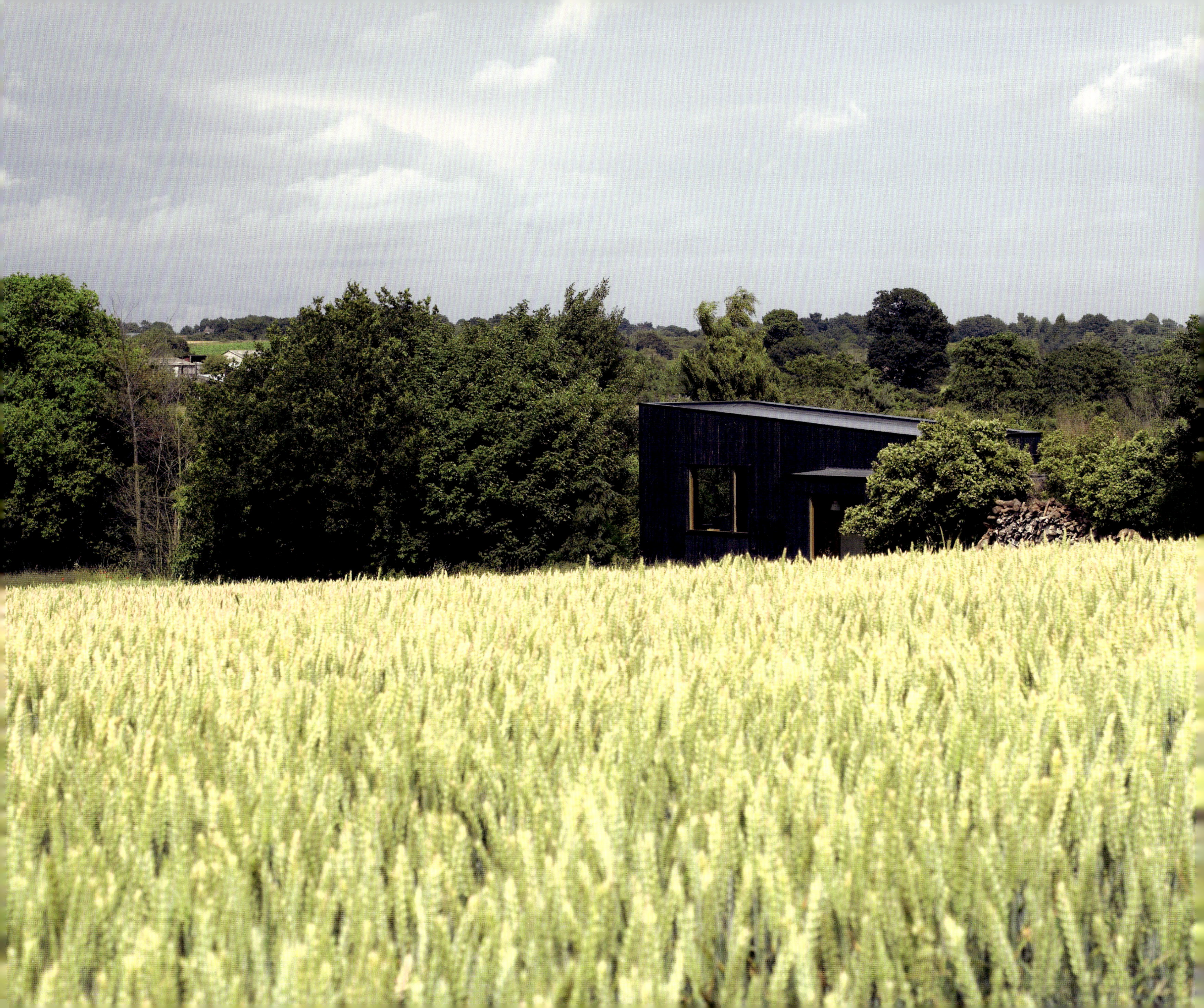

Right
The form of the house responds, in subtle ways, to the gentle shift in the topography.

Houses: Glen View

protected by a half-wall of joinery with bookcases embedded in the opposite flank. This sense of partial enclosure is accentuated through the fact that the entrance is a few steps lower than the main living space, meaning that one has to step upwards and inwards before the open-plan living area truly reveals itself.

Here, the reclaimed slate floors (sourced in Suffolk) unite the overall space, which features a seating area arranged around the wood burner, plus a small dining space and the bespoke kitchen with a long island, topped with iroko. Oak veneer panelling to dado height also helps to unify the space, while adding natural warmth and helping bring this high, open and spacious part of the home down towards the human scale. Importantly, such elements also add a crafted quality, along with the handmade kitchen. Ceiling lights floating over the kitchen island and dining table have a touch of Alvar Aalto about them, especially in combination with the light timber, yet were sourced from Habitat at an accessible price.

Moving towards the rear of the house, one passes the doorway to a separate pantry to one side of the kitchen and a set of French doors to a small, sheltered terrace. The space transforms into a narrower hallway as one continues through to the three bedrooms situated at the far end of the house, as it tucks into the gentle slope of the land. The long promenade through the house increases the perception of space and volume, yet the bedrooms offer private retreats by way of contrast.

In terms of budget Glen View encapsulates a different kind of brief compared to some of Gorst's other country houses, built to a larger scale and high specifications. Yet the results are, in many ways, just as pleasing and original, with the relative modesty of this English cabin working in its favour.

'I do think it's a lovely house and would be very happy living in it myself', says Gorst. 'It does demonstrate that you can build exciting and contemporary architecture at an affordable price without being elitist. That's very important, when you look around and see the quality of what's being built at the lower end of the housing market, especially in rural locations. There is no reason why every family shouldn't have a sitting room four and a half metres high and full of natural light. Everyone who comes into Glen View feels uplifted by it.'

Opposite
The cranked floor plan.

Below, left
From the kitchen sink towards the entrance – the low bookcase doubles as a protective balustrade.

Below
The inglenook with a vintage Jotul wood-burner. A datum of oak veneered ply panelling provides an intimate anchoring within a high-ceilinged white space.

Houses: Glen View

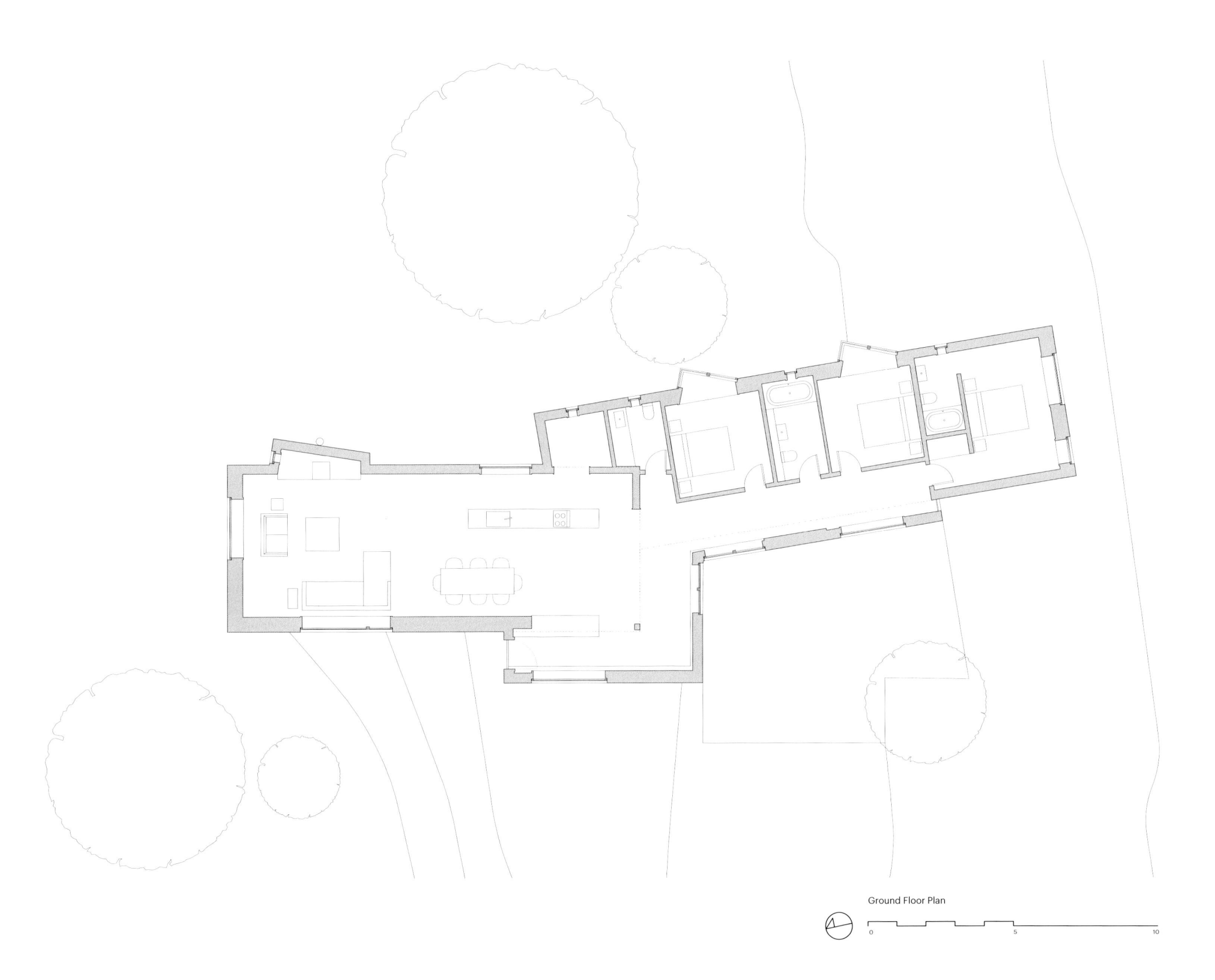

Ground Floor Plan

0　　　　　5　　　　　10

71

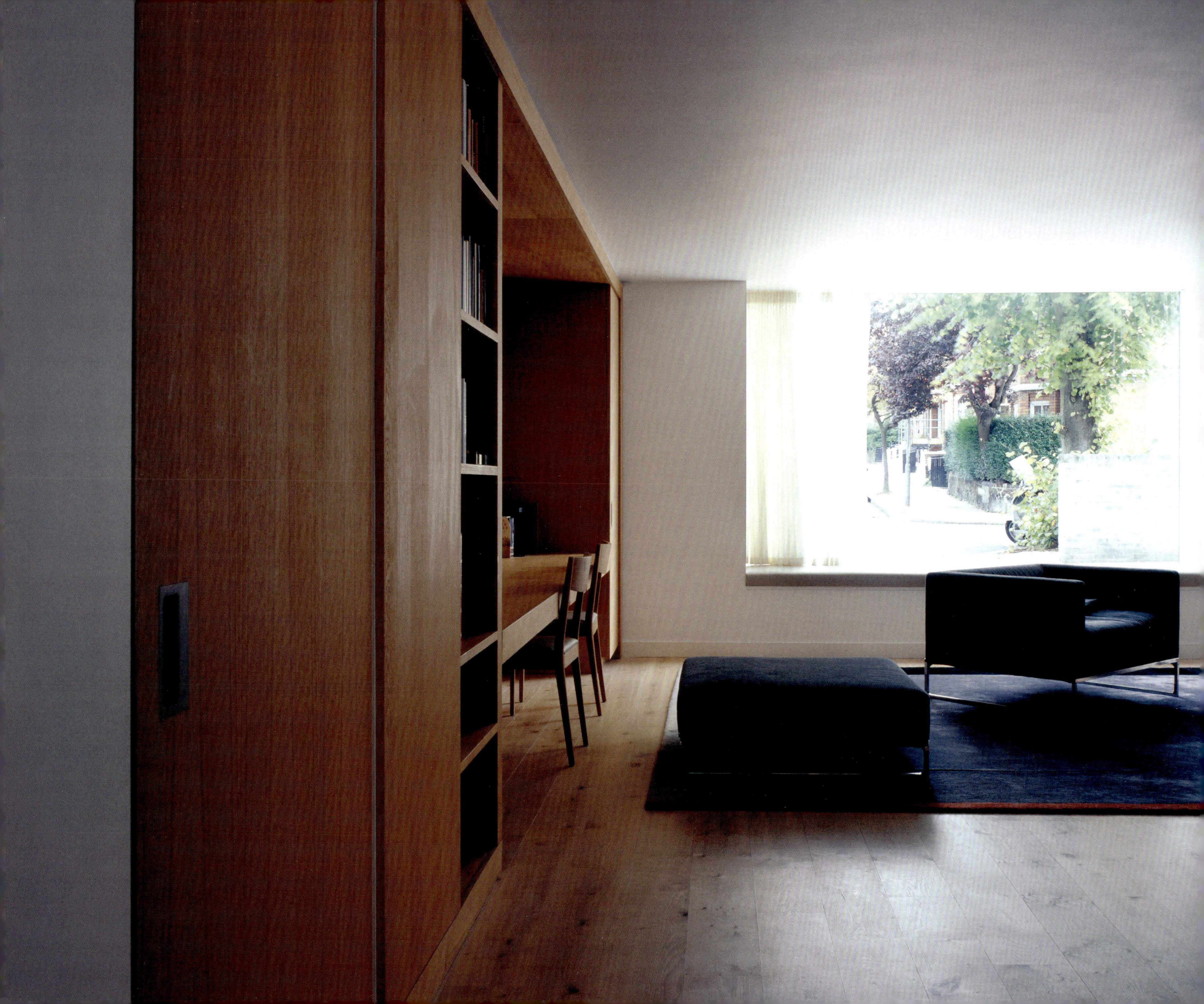

Leaf House

London
2010

Urban sites tend to carry with them a mass of planning restrictions and conditions, particularly in London. Yet the design and build of Leaf House offered an unusual degree of freedom, given that the north London site is not in a conservation area and the former dwelling that the new project replaced was of little merit or interest. The neighbouring buildings, too, are a mixture of early 20th-century residential blocks and post-war semi-detached houses. There was, therefore, little in the way of provenance within the site itself and significant latitude around the creative solution to a brief for a 21st-century family house for a couple with two young children who also work from home, each requiring a dedicated study.

'We didn't have any of those usual constraints of "fitting in"', says Gorst, who worked on Leaf House with project architect William Smalley. 'The streetscape here is very diverse and, to my mind, all the more interesting for that. So, the house takes its place unapologetically among its neighbours with no need for contextual deference. But it does connect to Georgian urban architecture in its sobriety, so for that reason it could be seen as a modern townhouse prototype of sorts in that it shares the austere restraint of some period terraced homes.'

The house steps back from the line of the street itself, with a courtyard forming a transitional zone to the private realm. The facade balances glazing (including generous picture windows) with a coating of Portland stone and a 'bay' of stainless-steel cladding around the front entrance and adjoining spaces.

On the ground floor a family den sits to the front and then the house begins to unfold as it stretches back on its long, thin site. A combined kitchen and dining area feeds out to a secret and walled garden to the rear, which also includes a separate garden pavilion – a flexible family space suited to a variety of uses.

The basement level is put to full use, accommodating not only a plant room and service spaces but also a large playroom for the children and a spacious study/library for one of the parents; skylights introduce natural light to both the study and the play space.

Moving upwards, the house begins to slim down, with three bedrooms and a children's bathroom on the first floor. The second floor is devoted to the master suite, which includes a bedroom, bathroom, dressing area and 'night cabin' – a more contemplative retreat overlooking the back garden. The top level hosts a pavilion on a smaller footprint – a treetop space raised above the rest of the building, which serves as the second study, or atelier, in Leaf House.

In this way, the working spaces are arranged at the base and summit of the home, separate not only from one another but from the everyday family living rooms. This arrangement offers quiet, contemplative studies, which are also tailored to the needs of the clients with fitted bookshelves, desks and storage.

Materially and ergonomically the house is both crafted and bespoke, tied to the particular needs of the family. There are many integrated pieces of furniture throughout, offering a pleasing level of cohesion but also making the most of the available space within this dense urban context, where every square foot has particular value in multiple senses of the word. The staircase is emblematic of the project as a whole – a key feature that carries you through the house via shifting volumes and light-filled spaces. The handrail is in tactile walnut, while the balusters are in lacquered steel.

'Leaf House has a dignified and timeless quality', says Gorst. 'Perhaps there are elements of Adolf Loos' villas within it and its pale, spectral tonal language. It has an intellectual austerity to it. But it's also about the combination of home and office for the young family that live in it. So, there's this fusion of life/work that demonstrates the increasing influence of information technology on the planning of the private house.'

Page 72–73
A framed view out towards the streetscape from the family room at the front of the house.

Above
From the kitchen towards the garden room.

Right
Entrance hall with walnut and lacquered steel balustrade on the staircase.

Right
The tripartite street facade –
stainless steel and Portland
stone capped by a leaf-patterned
attic glass pavilion.

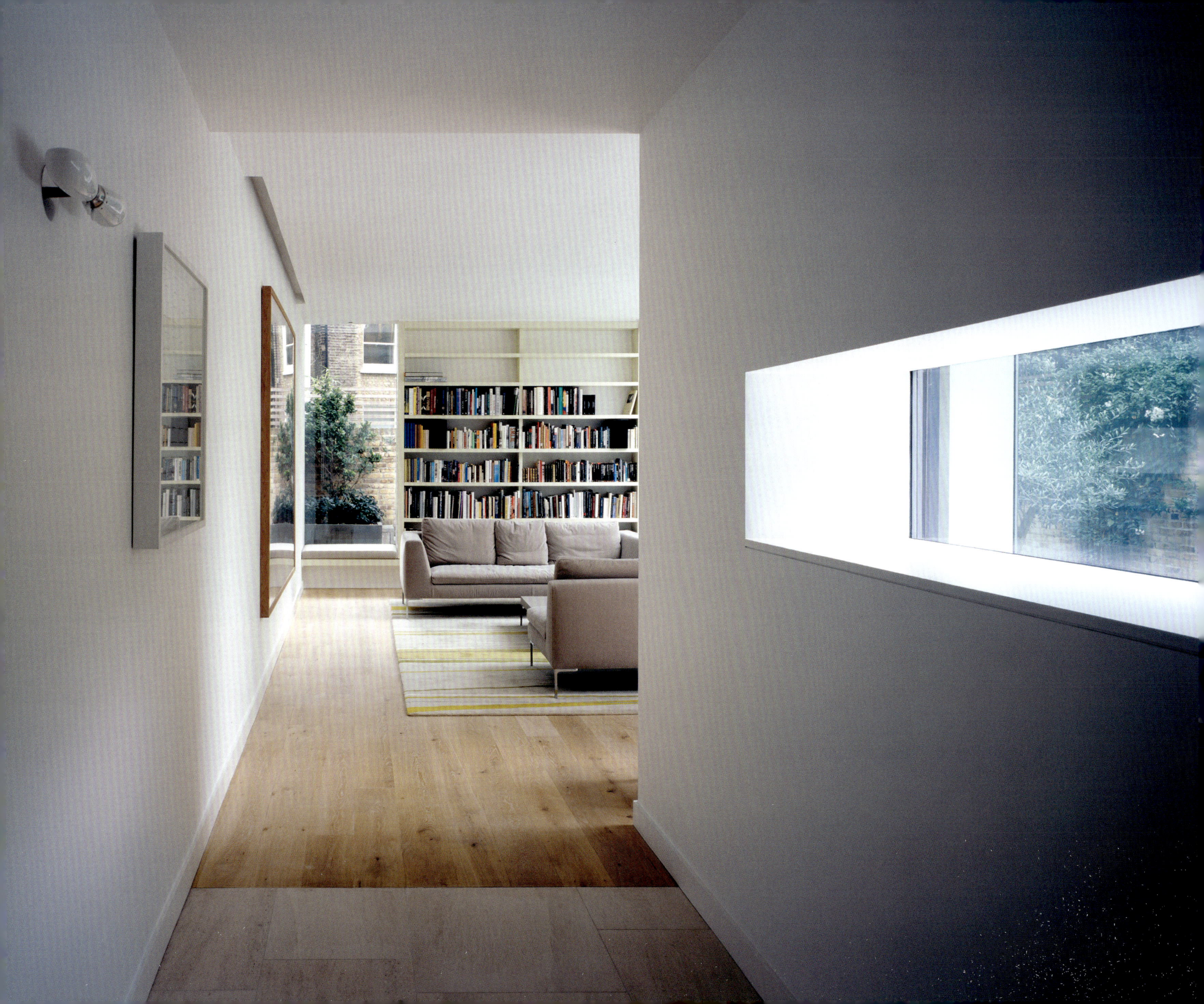

Opposite
A long horizontal cut in the wall enlivens the corridor.

Right
The unmediated planes and geometric intersections of the staircase hall. The acid etched glass of the entrance door is bottom right.

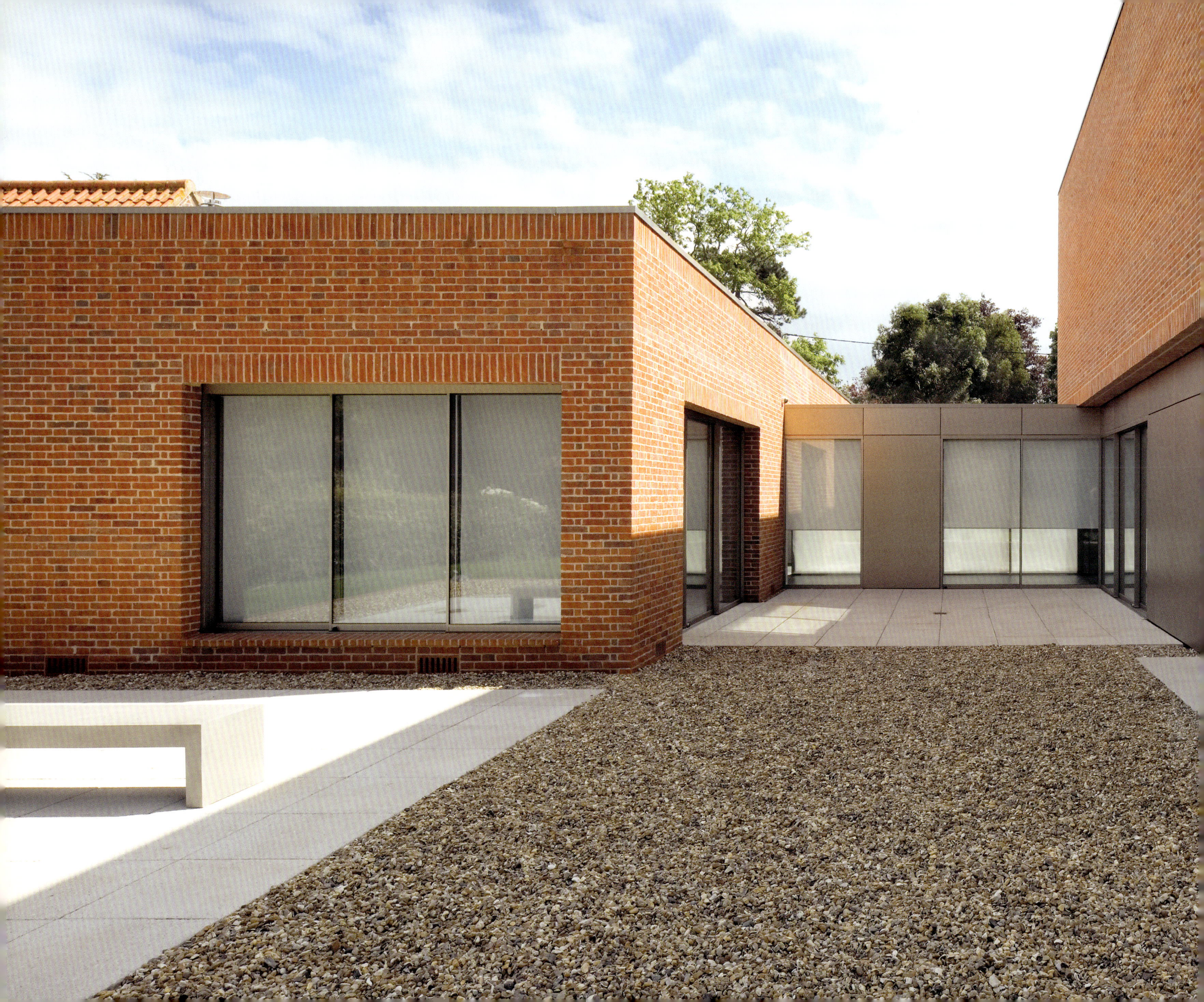

Brick House

Suffolk

2011

The Suffolk coastal town of Aldeburgh is picturesque and characterful. It was, famously, home to Benjamin Britten and – along with nearby Snape Maltings – hosts an annual arts festival. It is a place of music, history and culture but also sits upon a delightful stretch of coast that offers much in the way of natural beauty, particularly in combination with the open countryside that borders the town and draws you inland, as well as along the coastline.

James Gorst has a home in the county of Suffolk himself and a deep understanding of the county and its contexts, both coastal and rural. He was approached by a client who wanted to build a new holiday home on the edge of the town, which would offer accommodation for multiple generations of the same family. The new house replaces an existing building, using a similar footprint, while seeking to create a strong degree of privacy for the family. In this respect, the house offered a greater challenge than some of Gorst's other rural projects in more open settings, with sight lines to and from neighbouring houses a key consideration.

Gorst decided to orient the house towards the rear garden, which is bordered by mature trees that offer a green backdrop. The back garden becomes, in a way, an outdoor room in itself, with key parts of the house connecting directly to the outdoors via a hinterland of semi-sheltered courtyards and terraces.

Echoing the neighbouring houses, Gorst and his fellow director David Roy, decided to build the house with brick, deciding upon a local, handmade version from the Bulmer Brickyard, near Sudbury. It is a characterful brick, laid in traditional Flemish bond using lime mortar, yet the form of the house is precise, linear and very contemporary in comparison with the neighbours.

'I was tempted to build a fairly abstract modern house in this very traditional material', says Gorst. 'Brick does have many attractions – it's a familiar and enduring material that connects to a long architectural tradition and the "module" of the brick allows for such a wide range of textural, aesthetic and decorative alternatives. But it does also create a crafted quality in a building and that can be reassuring while also answering contemporary needs.'

The house itself spreads across the width of the site, clearly divided into two parts with one part arranged on just one level and the other set over two; a subtle, semi-transparent central link ties the two elements together. Facing the street nearby, the house appears largely closed and somewhat enigmatic, particularly in the lowermost portion of the building, which presents a closed wall of brick. The two-storey element achieves something more complex from this elevation,

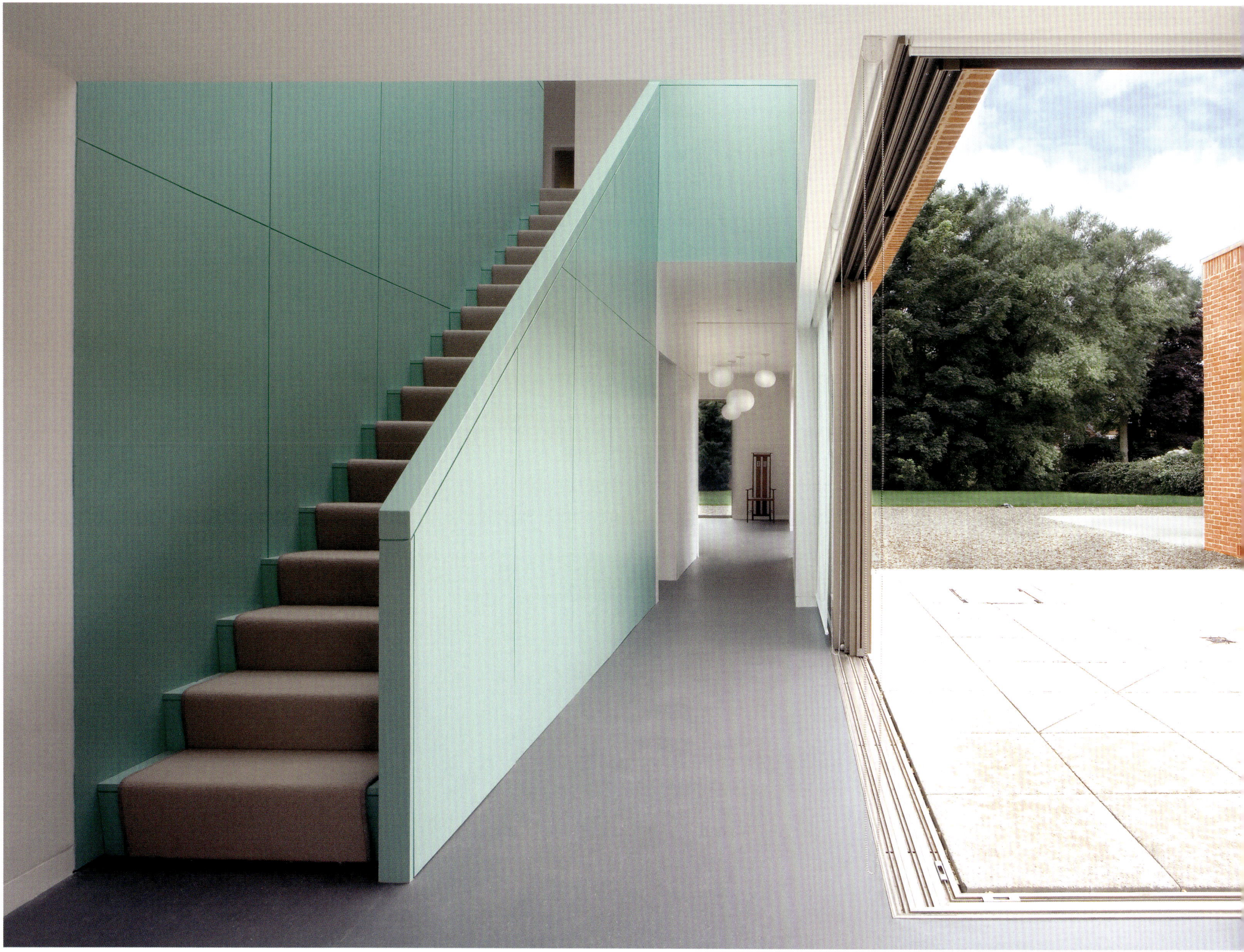

Pages 78-79
Brick House from the garden.

Left
An arsenic green stair drops down to the internal courtyard.

Below
A modernist celebration of hand-made bricks from Bulmer Brick and Tile Company laid in Flemish bond with a lime mortar.

as seen from the gravel driveway, with a brick box floating over a semi-transparent base level, featuring sheets of glass among insulated aluminium panels.

'The conceit behind this is that these two brick boxes have dropped down onto the site and one has landed and one is hovering', says Gorst. 'Juxtaposed with the houses nearby, it does look relatively alien, as least from the street, and it is rather provocative in some ways and uncompromising. But the material, certainly, is accessible and familiar.'

The single-storey element of the house features utility and storage spaces at its closed end and then opens up with a sequence of kitchen, dining and lounge areas, which connect with the courtyard and garden. The other part of the house offers a master suite at ground level, along with a more formal sitting room looking out onto the garden. Upstairs there are four further bedrooms, offering spaces for all members of the family.

To the rear garden, the house features much more in the way of sliding glass, allowing a degree of transparency and a blurring of the boundaries between inside and out. In this respect, there is a vivid contrast with the more enclosed elevation to the front. A small timber pavilion in the back garden provides a games room and den for the younger generation.

For Gorst himself, there is a degree of synergy between Brick House and Sandpipers in the use of geometric, rectangular forms that are then eroded in one way or another. The contexts and the choice of materials are clearly very different, with brick for one and timber cladding for the other, yet they also both explore the use of traditional materials in unexpected and contemporary ways.

Above
The street elevation.

Below
Ground and first floor plans.
Two volumes umbilically linked
by the glazed entrance hall.

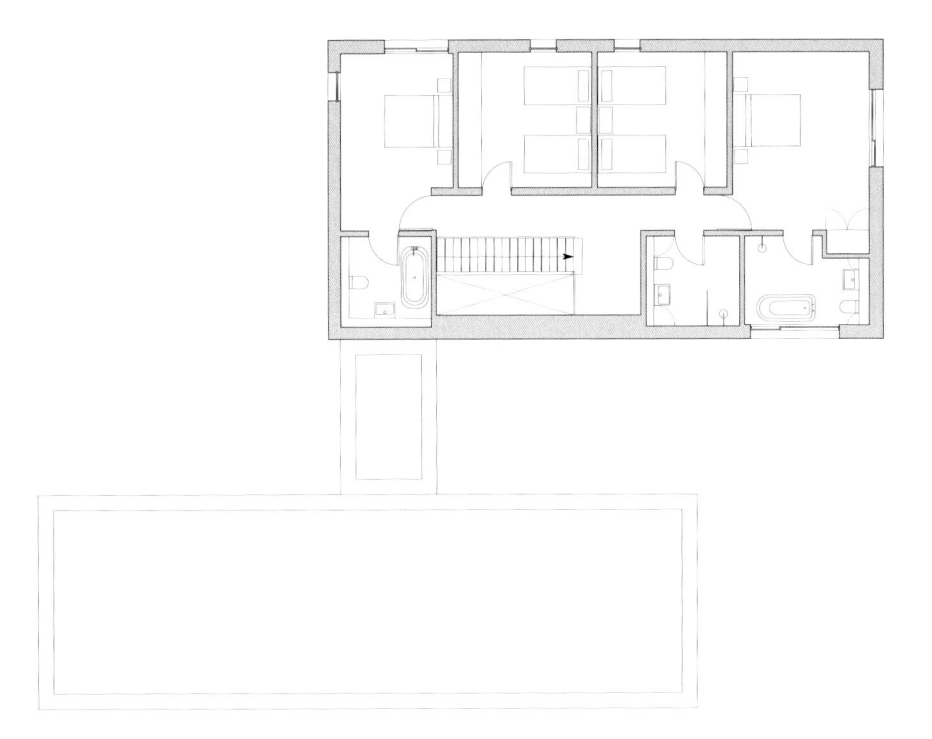

Houses: Brick House

First Floor Plan

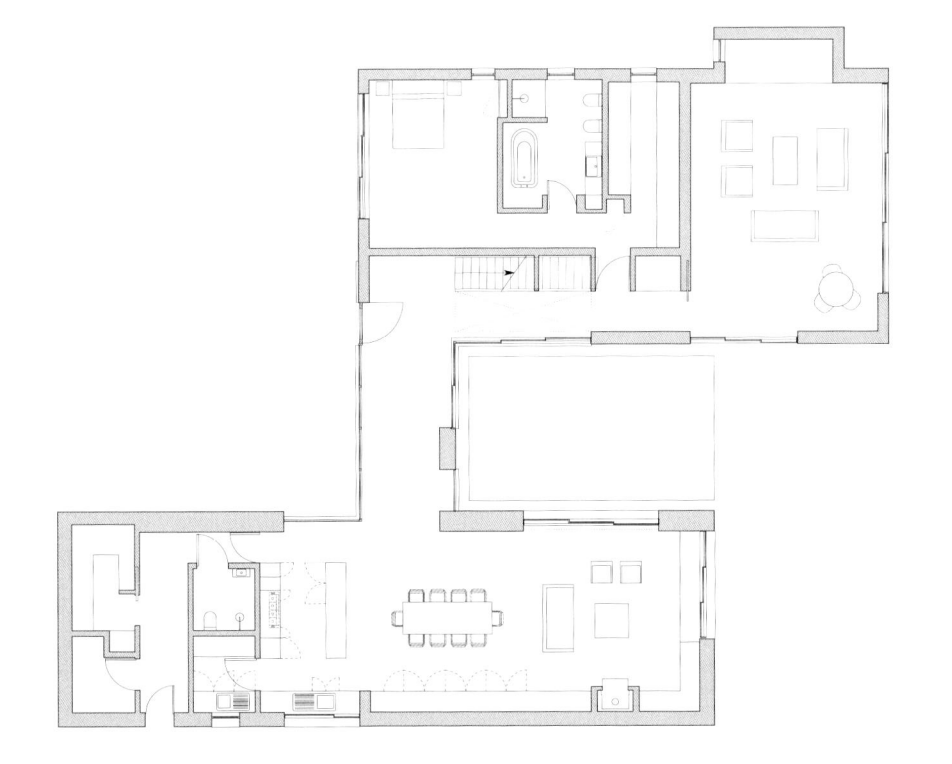

Ground Floor Plan

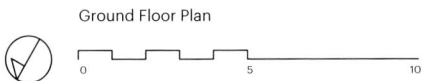

83

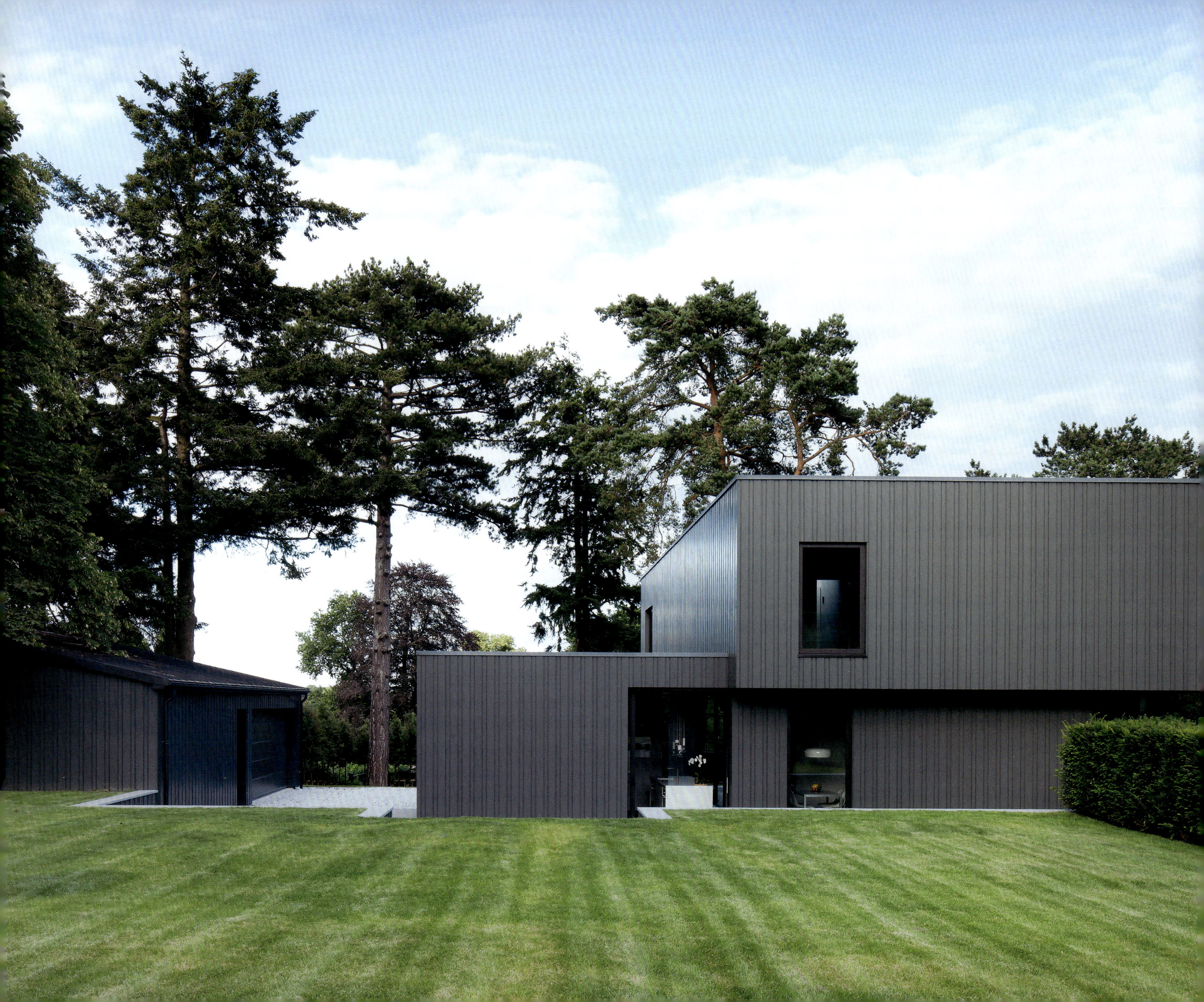

Sandpipers

Surrey
2016

Perched on top of a ridge on the edge of the South Downs, Sandpipers makes the most of its high vantage point. The house looks out over the countryside, dotted with small villages and farmhouses nestling among the trees, with picture windows framing key views of the landscape. From the sitting room and dining room, in particular, expanses of floor to ceiling glass offer a vivid relationship with this open vista.

'When you are in spaces such as the dining room, which has a glass corner, you do have this lovely feeling of expansion and openness,' says Gorst. 'It is a wonderful position up on the hill, looking out over lush water meadows and the meandering river girded by trees. It really is lovely and the house responds to it, of course, and connects with the landscape.'

James Gorst's client had nurtured a wish to build a contemporary, bespoke home for many years. A civil servant, he had first noticed Gorst's work when a planning application for a country house designed by the architect was called into the department where he was working. Later, when the family were ready to build something for themselves, they got in touch.

The site was originally occupied by a bungalow dating from the Sixties, which was replaced by the new, two storey building, sitting on the same footprint as the original house while expanding slightly upon it. The client re-landscaped around the house, planting more trees along the driveway to add to the mature pines. A separate garage and store alongside the house helps to define the approach to the front door, while there is also a small pavilion alongside the swimming pool in the garden. All three structures feature precision-made timber cladding, stained a soft grey, creating a degree of synergy between the triptych.

The house itself is linear, formed of two interlocking boxes, which subverts the precision of the rectangle at various points, adding character and interest. A single storey element projects outwards to one side, helping to define the entry 'courtyard' outside, while also containing the kitchen and utility spaces. The lower box is indented and eroded on one elevation and the upper box cantilevers outwards slightly over the lower on others, creating subtle shifts in the geometry, while also helping to shelter key areas such as the main entrance.

Stepping inside, one enters a spacious hallway with the oak staircase to one side. Elsewhere on the ground floor, Gorst purposefully avoids any other circulation corridors, opting instead for an enfilade of inter-connected living spaces that invite a journey through the house, passing from one space to another. It is a characteristic approach, common to Gorst's work as a whole. 'One of my central preoccupations in designing houses and interiors is to get away from corridors, unless it's a really interesting space with a wonderful window or doorway at the end of it,' says Gorst. 'But generally they are dull and neglected spaces. Obviously you can't walk from one bedroom into another, so landings are needed for privacy, but elsewhere there is no need and I prefer a "promenade architecturale". The liberation of the kitchen, which is no longer tucked away at the back of the house, has helped with this and provides a more open and informal floor plan. But in houses like Sandpipers you still have these little areas of privacy as well, such as the little study just off the library.'

The enfilade offers a sequence of key living spaces, namely the library, the central sitting room and the dining room, which – in turn – connects with the kitchen. Recessed pocket doors offer the option to separate one space from another, as required, providing a degree of flexibility for the family.

The library features bespoke book shelves and storage, made in oak, while timber panelling is used in the dining room, helping to add a craft element but also introducing natural textures. Literal and implied warmth is also provided by the fireplace in the sitting room, offering a key focal point and underlining the continuing importance of the hearth in Gorst's residential projects.

Upstairs, there are five bedrooms. Here, one truly floats above the landscape, looking down upon the valley below. Bathrooms are generally located at the centre of the floor plan, but illuminated with skylights, drawing out the character of the marble, which has been used extensively. With the landing, Gorst has been careful to avoid wasting an opportunity, using the space as a 'room' or gallery in itself, with fitted benches and banks of storage. A long skylight helps make the space welcoming, adding to the wealth of light that percolates through every part of Sandpipers.

Pages 84–85
Bordered by mature trees, the house makes the most of the natural setting and vantage point.

Below
The entry courtyard is defined by the projecting kitchen wing, garage and mature pine trees.

Opposite
Vignettes of the drive, the stair and the drawing room from the marble kitchen.

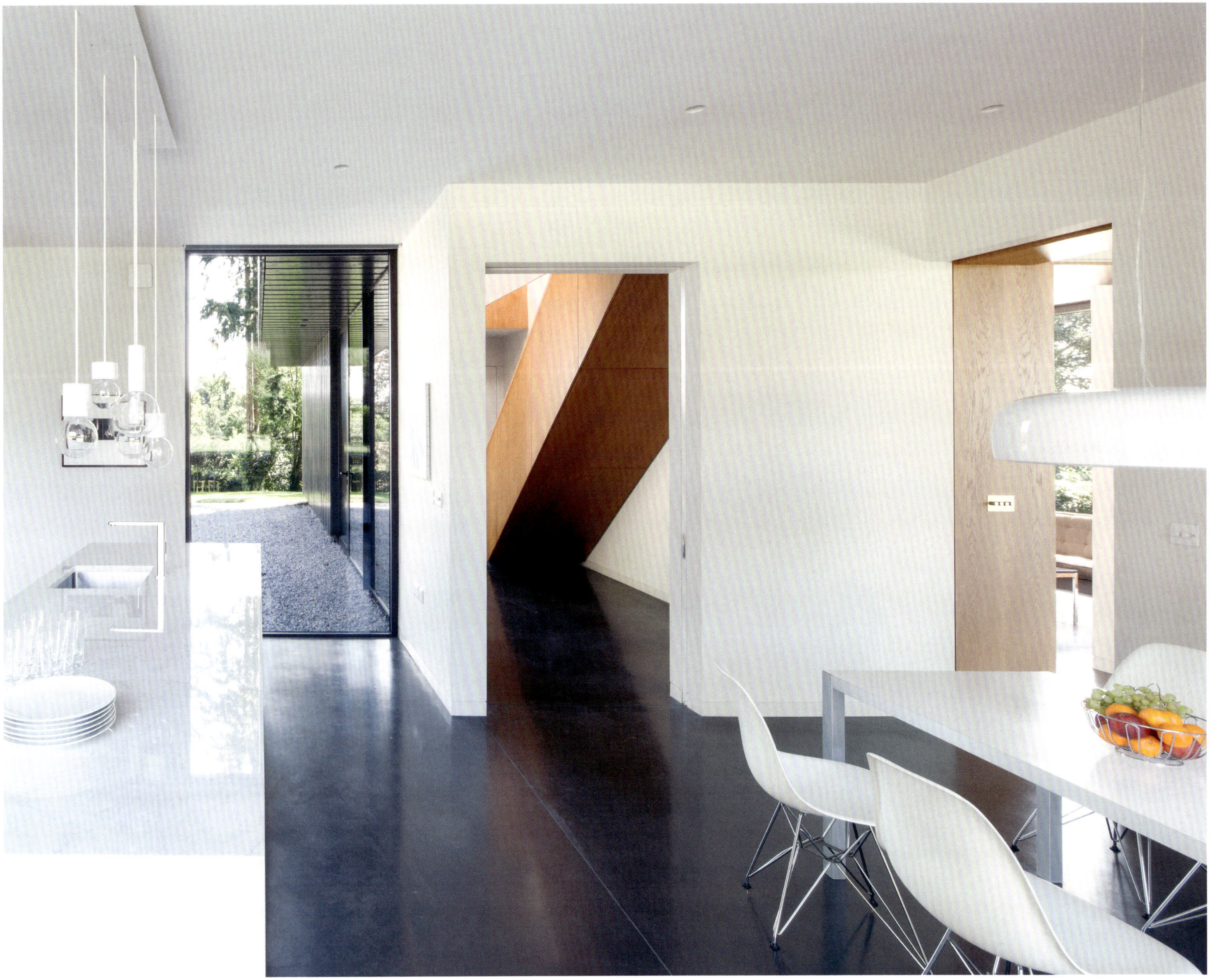

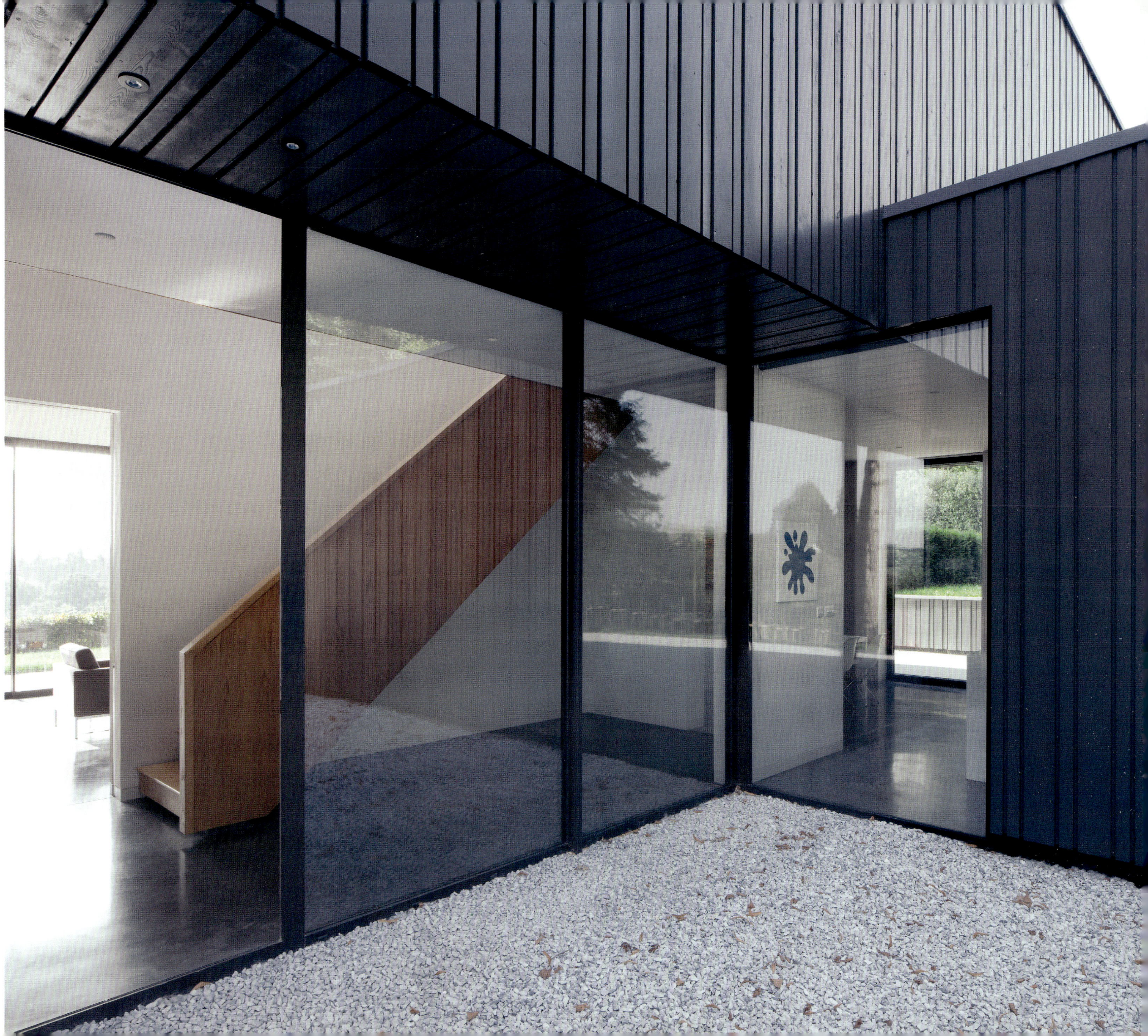

Opposite
The point of entry.

Right
Generous seating and storage spaces line one side of the top-lit landing.

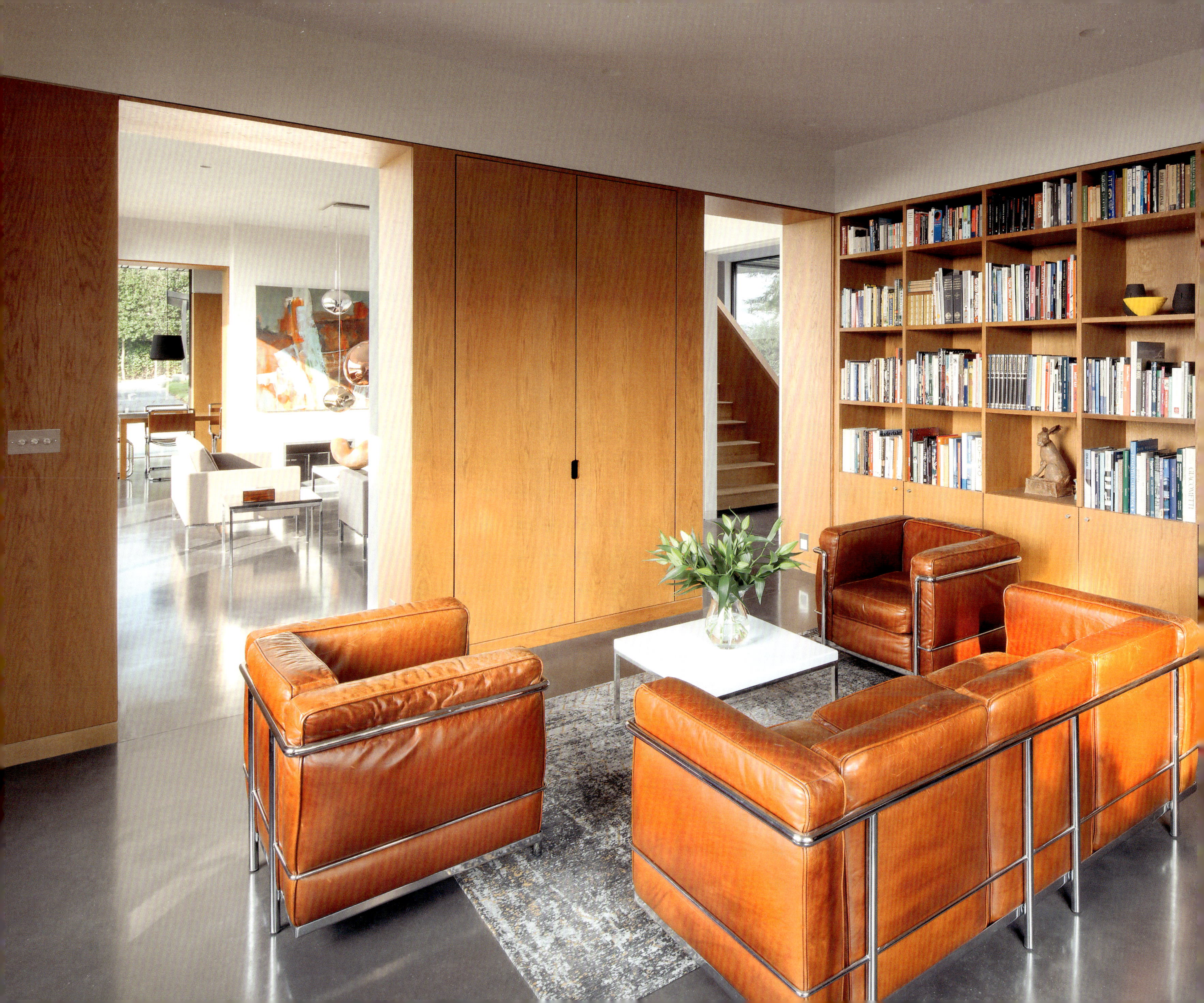

Opposite
From the library to the drawing room with the dining room beyond – the full sequence of reception rooms.

Above
White walls, polished concrete floors and oak – a restrained, consistent palette unifies the interior.

The Timeless Home

Right
The ground and first floor plan.

Opposite
The slipped first floor overhang shelters the large corner window overlooking the lush pastoral below.

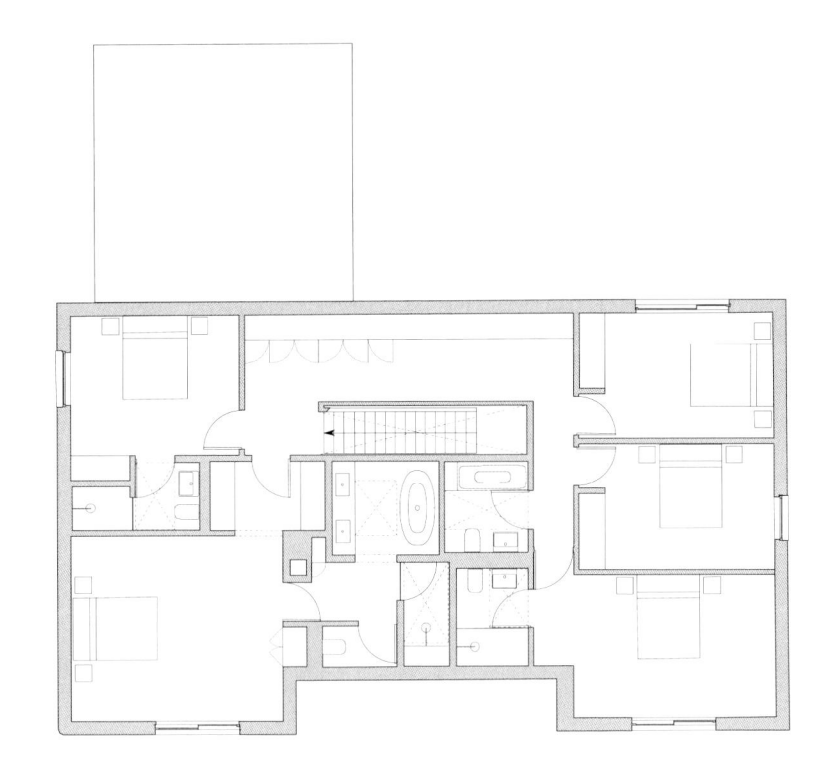

First Floor Plan

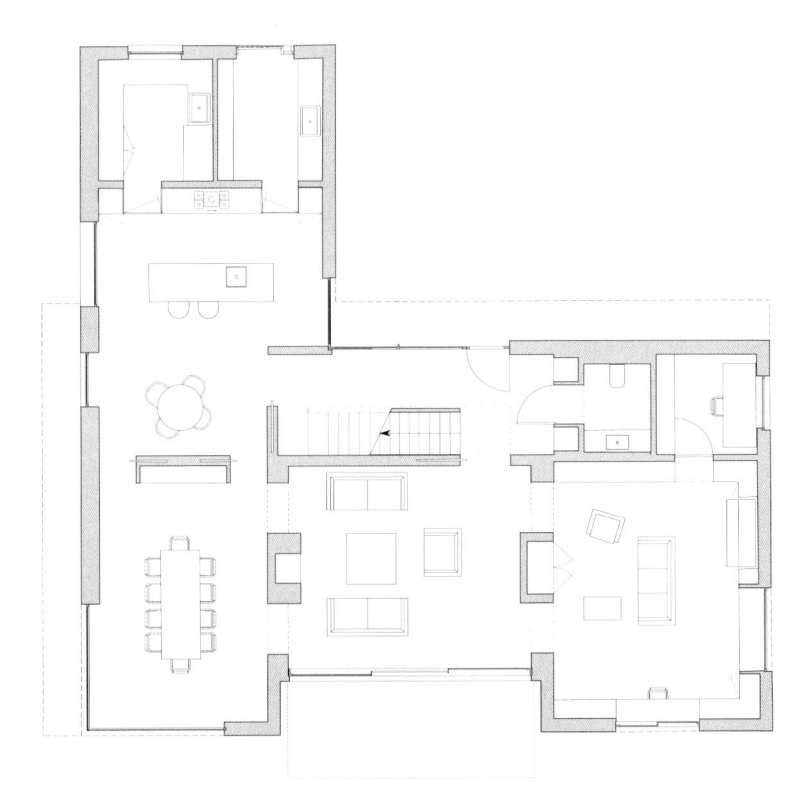

Ground Floor Plan

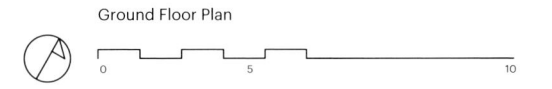

Houses: Sandpipers

Reinventions and Adaptations

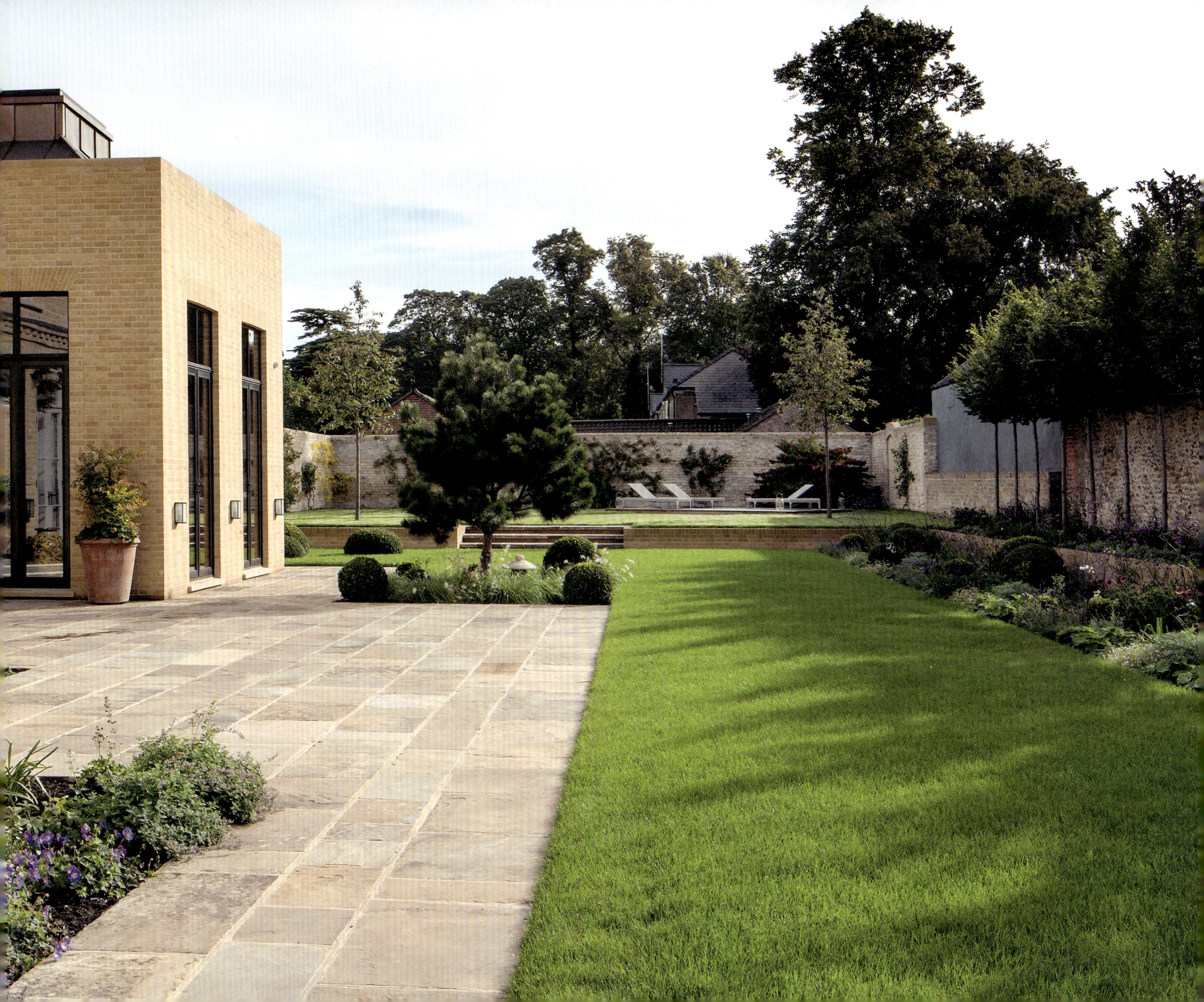

Reinventions and Adaptations

Houses do not stand still. They evolve and change over time, according to the needs and preoccupations of their owners as well as shifting patterns of everyday living. A period home will, quite commonly, have been extended and altered many times over the course of its lifetime, creating a kind of architectural diary lasting many centuries. Not all of these changes, of course, will have been for the best and many contemporary restoration programmes and updates begin by attempting to read this diary and – often – sweep away the mistakes of the past, with lean-tos and conservatories grafted on during the 1960s and 1970s often the first to go.

James Gorst has read these diaries with care. As noted in his foreword to this book, during the early part of his career in the 1980s, many of his projects involved the 'refurbishment of battered and abused Georgian terraced houses that had fallen victim to multiple occupation'. Gorst's task at that time was often 'more of a picture restorer than a painter', as he sought to bring back a sense of unity and order to such homes, undoing the errors of the past, while working to fill in the many gaps created by the removal of period elements and key features over the years. At the same time, the imperative was to make these homes fit for modern living and suited to our more casual, informal and fluid lifestyles.

Such projects were valuable in the evolution of Gorst's own methodology, which has always been based on respect. This applies not only to a building in itself, but also to those who first designed and made it, for the artisans and craftsmen who laid the floors or fashioned the staircase, for those who made and fitted the fireplaces or created the plaster mouldings for the ceilings. Beyond this, there is a respect for the broader context of the neighbourhood, village or town and its own unique vernacular. All of these elements are part of the story of house and home.

Within the many reinventions, restorations and adaptations undertaken by Gorst and his practice, there is a recognition that the work in hand is the next important step within a gradual, evolutionary process of change. Many such projects involve listed buildings but there is, in any event, always a level of care and understanding that places respect at the heart of the process.

One of the most important and rewarding such projects, for Gorst and his colleagues, was the restoration and extension of Wakelins in Suffolk. This period farmhouse had already been adapted and extended many times, growing over time as two farm workers' cottages were fused together, then extended in the 19th century and then changed again during the 1970s. The diary here was long and complex, while the level of ambition from the client – who wanted a substantial country house suited to 21st-century living – was very high.

Wakelins was a multi-layered project full of different challenges within an overall master plan that brought new order and legibility to the house. There was the careful restoration and update of the original parts of the building, plus a period barn alongside. There was also a substantial new addition at one end of the house, offering an enticing new sitting room at ground level and a master suite above.

Importantly, Gorst made a very clear distinction throughout between new and old. As one travels through Wakelins, there is no confusion regarding provenance, with Gorst always careful to avoid anything that smells of pastiche or dishonesty. The architectural historian can, if they wish, read the story of the house with great clarity.

Projects such as Wakelins and others on the following pages require an array of different skills and talents. Here, picking up on Gorst's own metaphor, the architect is both picture restorer and painter at one and the same time. The

Pages 94–95
Hurworth House.

original parts of a building are restored and updated, with modern services introduced, including lighting, heating and plumbing along with fresher technologies and amenities.

Additional elements are full of imagination, offering original and valuable features in their own right, as seen at Wakelins, Downs House and Hurworth House, with a respectful distinction made between the new and the old. Subtle and discreet links tend to create a degree of visual (not literal) separation between the elements, so the period and the contemporary can be read for what they are and appreciated on their own terms.

Such additions are decidedly modern, but also contextual in their own way. The sculptural form of the new studio at Downs House in Stoke-by-Nayland was, for example, inspired by the high-pitched roof of the original farmhouse, with similar clay roof tiles used to coat the body of this new chapter in its story.

Crucially all of these elements, both new and old, have to work together within a logical, functional master plan. Gorst has never been afraid to take some radical decisions in order to create a house that really works for modern living, as can be seen at Hurworth House in Newmarket, where the practice had to reorder much of the internal floor plan of the original 19th-century house in order to strip away countless corridors and wasted, cellular spaces. At the same time, Gorst also designed a sympathetic new addition that provides a dramatic, spacious new focal point.

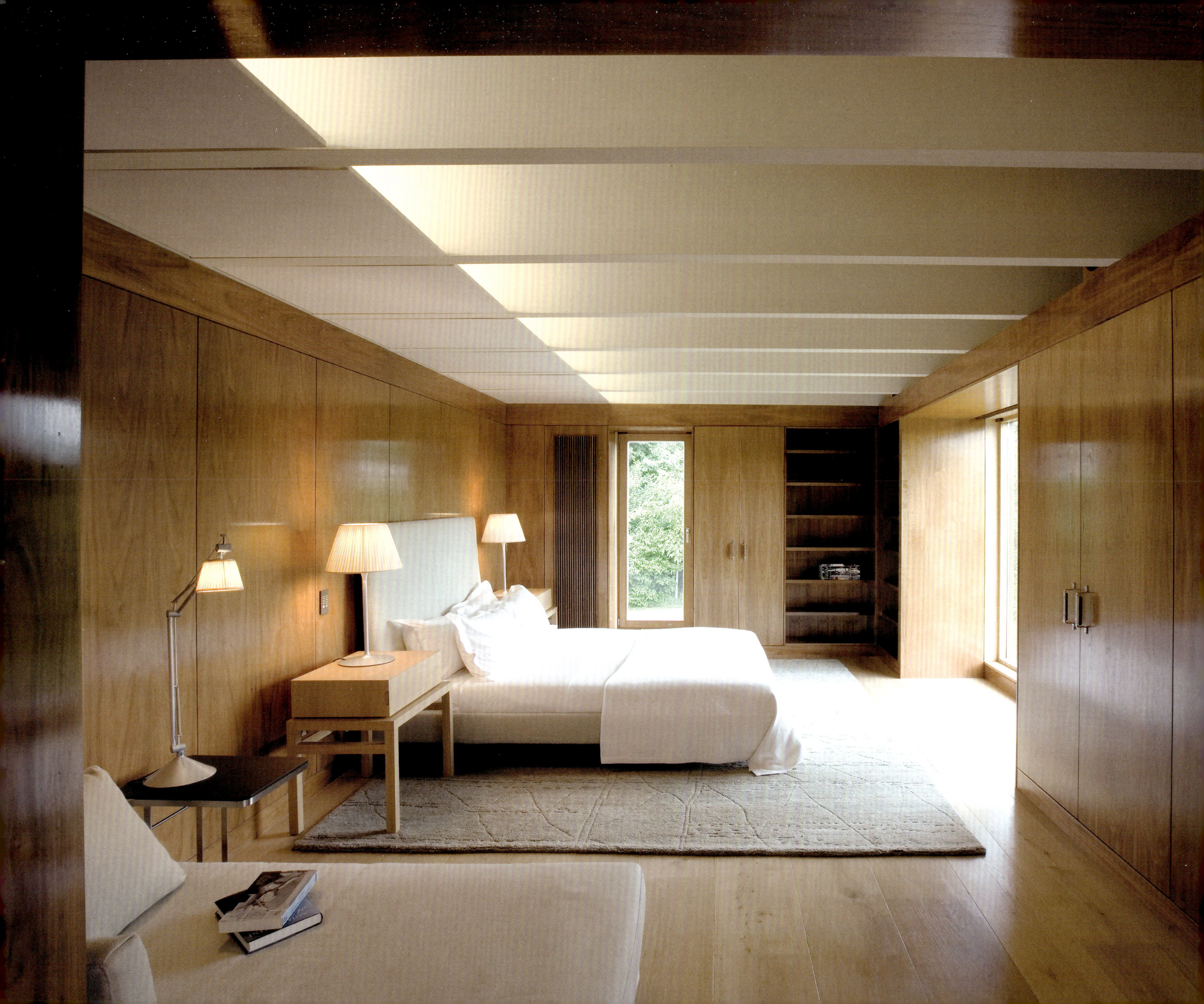

Wakelins

Suffolk
2003

The restoration, adaptation and extension of Wakelins represents, James Gorst suggests, one of the happiest and most satisfying projects of his architectural life to date. The project offered many challenges but the combination of an enlightened client, a delightful setting and a brief that included almost every detail from architecture through to furniture and beyond, helped in the creation of a home that is not only characterful but also rounded and cohesive. The new addition to the original Tudor farm buildings was, in particular, highly rewarding and almost has the feel of a house in its own right with a distinctly modern identity.

'It was one of the first times in my career when I thought I had actually created a piece of modern architecture that truly satisfied me, as well as the client', says Gorst. 'It's a modestly sized addition but one of the first buildings where I found a kind of expression that was asymetrical, with a lot of complex internal modulations of space with single and double height volumes. So I was proud of Wakelins for many personal reasons because the achievement of this relatively small building encapsulated a lot of the ideas I wanted to explore. It also ended up on the front cover of Alain de Botton's book *The Architecture of Happiness*, so I think people responded to it favourably.'

Gorst already knew the client well, having designed a home and offices for him in London. He acquired a crumbling Tudor farmhouse, with an 18th-century barn alongside, in a Suffolk village not far from Newmarket and Bury St Edmunds within an area that the architect knows well. The house itself was an amalgamation of a number of smaller farm workers' cottages that had been spliced and extended in Victorian times and then extended with lean-to additions during the 1970s.

The Grade II listed house offered a wonderful rural aspect and sat within extensive gardens. But as Gorst began to strip away the 1970s additions a whole series of problems with the Tudor structure revealed themselves. The oak frame had rotted over the years and just under half of it needed repair and careful re-patching, while it also transpired that there were no proper foundations, meaning that the frame had to be re-supported while new foundations were slotted in underneath it.

'At the beginning I don't think any of us had any notion of the amount of building work and restoration that we would need to do on the original part of the house', says Gorst. 'We effectively rebuilt the Tudor house and the challenge was to do this restoration work of the very highest quality and then add the contemporary piece that was unapologetically modern.'

Gorst took the opportunity during the rebuild of the Tudor portion to introduce contemporary services to a very high specification, while drawing on traditional building techniques and the skills of local craftsmen. Even in the old section of the building, Gorst makes a strong distinction between old and new, as seen in the entry hall – for example – where the wood burner and the oak panelling around it are clearly identifiable as an intervention, with a similar approach in the kitchen and dining area alongside. Beyond this, one moves to a separate music room and then into the semi-transparent and subservient linking zone to the new part of the project, with the intention – once again – of clearly marking the shift from old to new within an elongated sequence of structures that forms a rural terrace of interrelated elements.

The new addition, which is also two storeys, takes a degree of inspiration from Louis Kahn's Esherick House in Philadelphia (1961), which also offered a linear, modern form in combination with crafted interiors, as well as internal shifts in volume. Gorst takes a rectangular outline and pushes one portion of it a little past the other, with a double atrium towards the centre looking out onto reflecting pools. The modern addition has been clad in timber, softening the exterior, while the geometry has been undermined further by two eroded corners filled with glass.

The lower floor of the addition features a new sitting room/library, overlooking the gardens, and a study alongside. The upstairs segment holds the master suite, with another three bedrooms situated on the upper level of the Tudor farmhouse. There is much in the way of integrated, crafted elements such as bookcases, panelling, storage cupboards, dressing tables and so on. This helps to both simplify and unify the space, as well as adding to the overall functionality of Wakelins.

'It is wonderful to conceive a building like this and then see the execution right through to the moment where you can sit

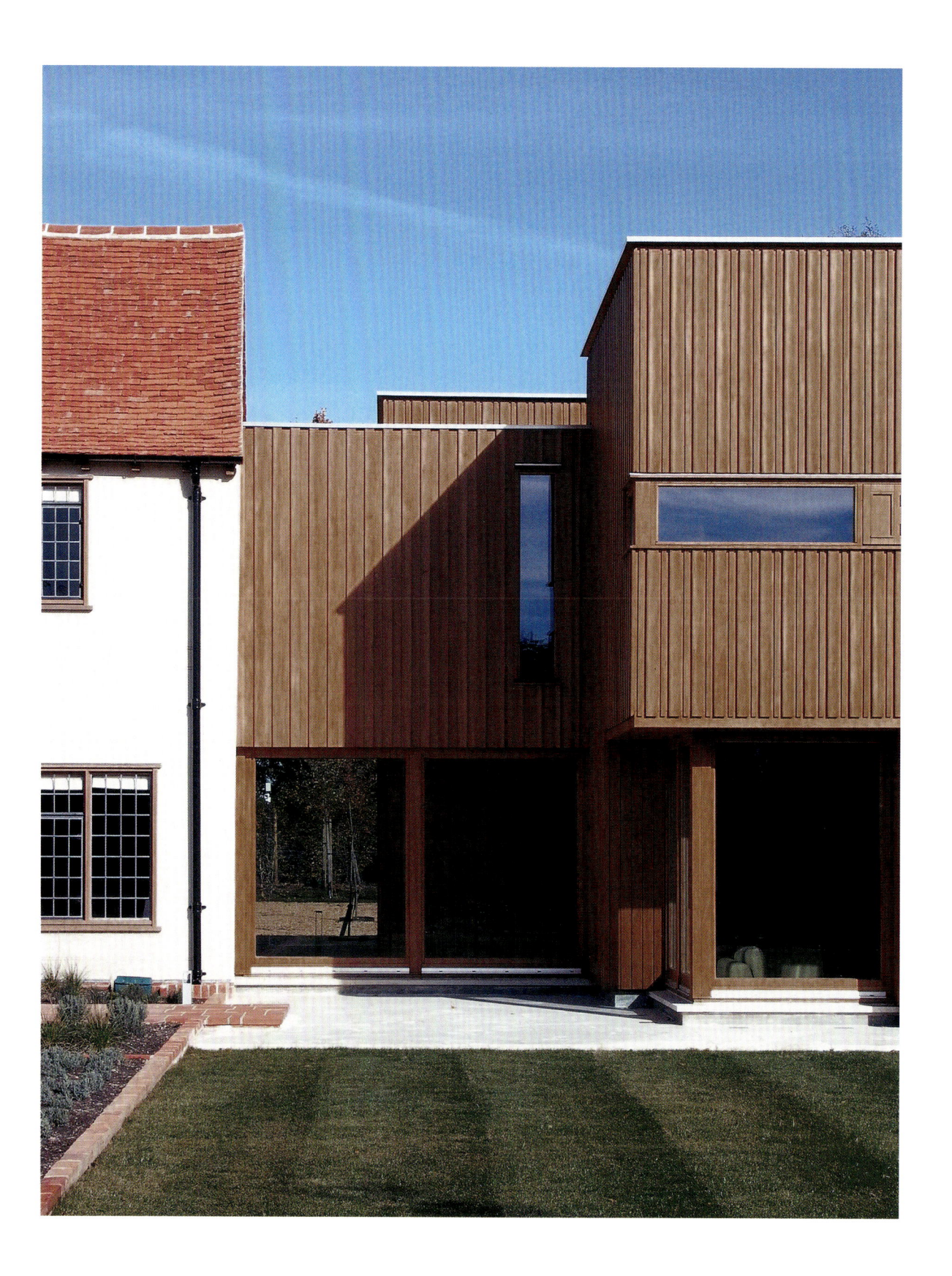

Pages 98–99
The main bedroom – French-polished walnut and a beamed ceiling.

Opposite
The junction of two forms of timber framed domestic architecture separated by 500 years.

Right
The rebuilt house – new chimneys with Tudor dimensioned hand-made bricks, pargetted lime plaster and oak casements with leaded lights. The new oak clad extension extends the linear plan.

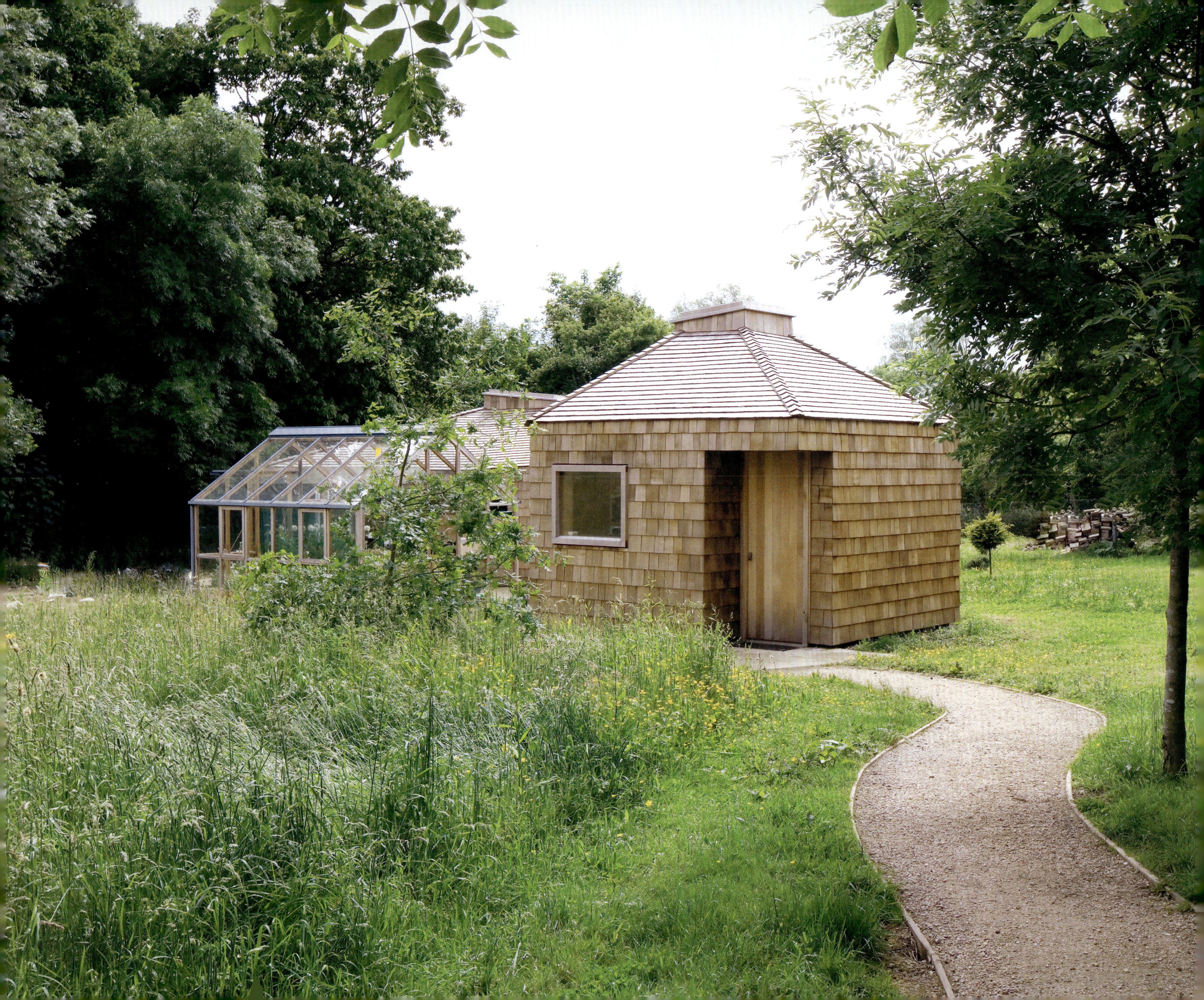

down in a fully complete space', says Gorst. 'There is no discord and nothing out of place, although that does all involve a lot of trust from the client. Responding to the landscape was also very important, especially within the design of the extension, which is almost like a crafted piece of furniture in itself.'

The project also included the restoration and adaptation of the barn alongside the house, principally for the use of a housekeeper, and – later on – the creation of a series of garden buildings known as Wakelins Meadows. This playful 'gardener's world' sits alongside the vegetable garden, with a shingle-clad workshop and storage shed for the gardener, as well as a greenhouse. This micro-cluster has the feel of a small settlement in itself, complementing the main residence and barn.

Opposite
A shingle office at the end of the garden.

Left
Scalloped oak boarding to catch the sun.

Left
The new main stair and window.

Below
A Conran chair by the new stair and staircase window.

Right
A base bed, Portland stone floor and English oak panelling.

The Timeless Home

Opposite
The design of the house offers a striking contrast between new and old, with the junction between them downplayed and reduced in height and scale to create a respectful point of union.

Below
The 19th- and 20th-century lean-to extensions were demolished from the original farmhouse to create a well-lit series of interlinking double aspect rooms. The aesthetic of the new extension creates an interesting dialogue with the preceding half-timbered interiors.

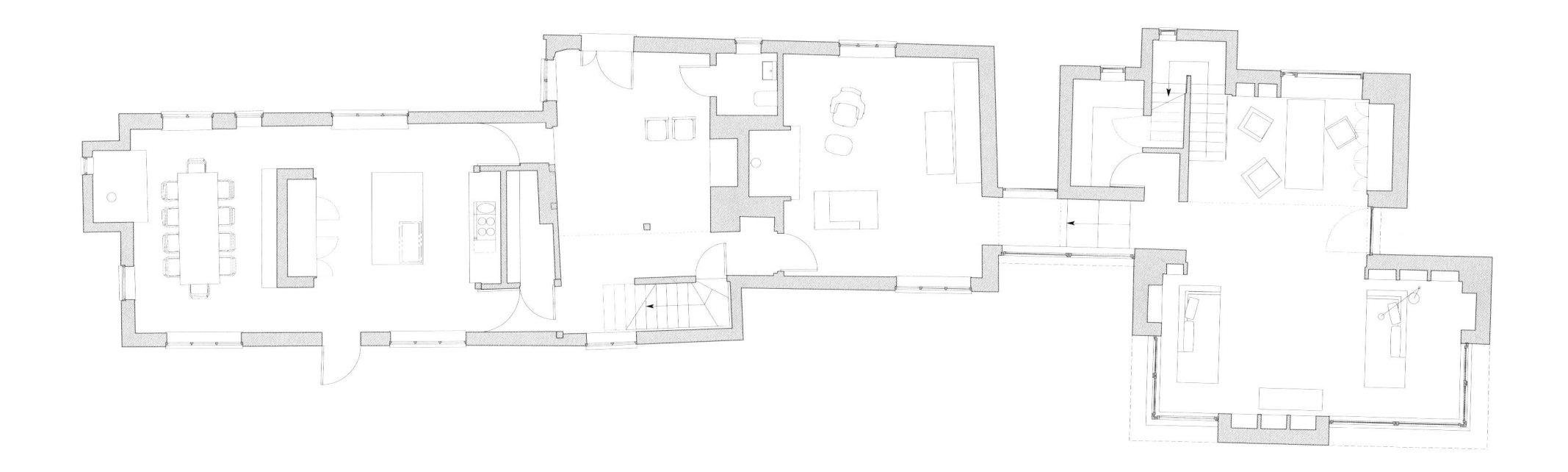

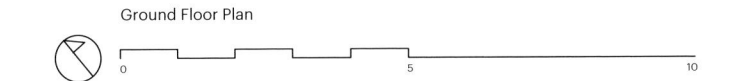

Ground Floor Plan

0   5   10

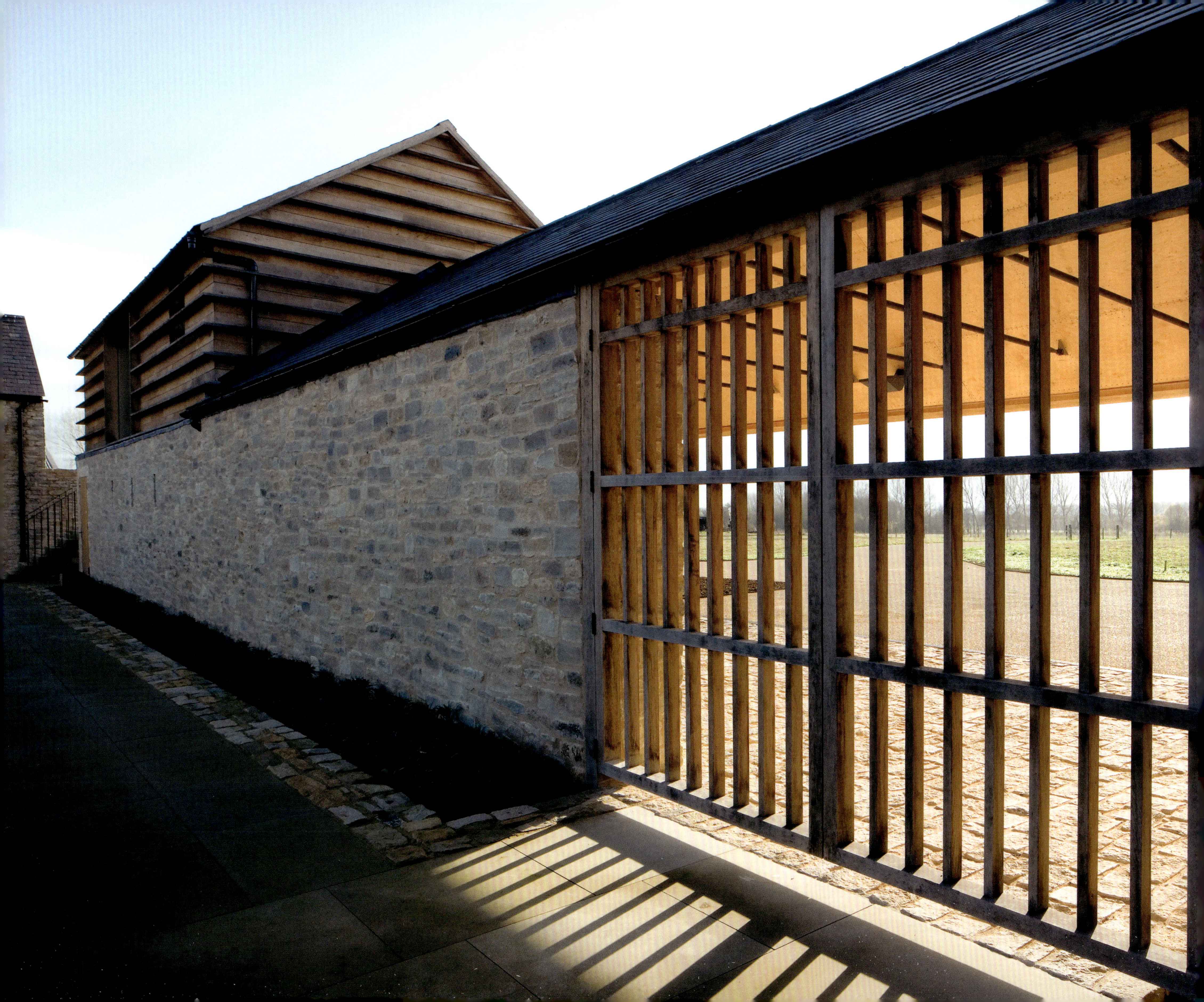

Watergate

Oxfordshire
2009 – 14

Situated in a rural part of Oxfordshire, Watergate encompasses a five-year project focused on the reinvention of a traditional farmstead into a compound of buildings devoted to art and everyday living. The clients – an artist and a jeweller – had owned the property for many years and one of the barns had previously been converted in the 1970s by the respected architects Peter Aldington and John Craig.

Working with project architect William Smalley, Gorst began the project with a master plan for the farmstead, which included sweeping away a number of peripheral agricultural sheds to improve the approach to the property, consisting of a farmhouse and barns, made of Cotswold stone, arranged around a farmyard. This central yard became a pivotal part of the scheme as a whole, transformed into a private quadrangle with stone pavers. The combination of the courtyard and a 'campus' of buildings echoes a university college, as well as the farmstead, with a large, open 'room' sitting at the very centre of the site.

The practice divided the project into two distinct parts. The first phase involved the conversion of a barn into a spacious, double-height art studio with a large glass window filling the old cart doorway to one side. The barn was largely rebuilt and restored, with vast sliding timber shutters to protect the glass as needed plus lime floors within, as well as a mezzanine for storing canvases.

The first phase also involved the creation of a new two-storey building, filling a gap around the central court. The ground floor section holds storage and garaging, while the upper level offers staff accommodation within a self-contained apartment; additional car ports and a double gateway either side help to further enclose and protect the courtyard.

This completely new building, in stone and timber, picks up on the vernacular context and particularly the farmstead typology, drawing upon an agrarian aesthetic. Yet the addition is also clearly contemporary, with a degree of inspiration taken from the rustic modern style of Swiss architect Peter Zumthor. The building is coated in oak fins, rather like a series of bookshelves, that lend character and a subtle suggestion of difference and distinction. An outdoor stone staircase to one side leads up to the staff apartment, which benefits from elevated views of the landscape to one side and the yard to the other.

The second phase involved the three-storey farmhouse itself and the stone barn alongside it, which had previously been converted by Aldington & Craig. The barn itself was updated with an open entertaining space on the lower floor and guest accommodation above. The practice introduced a new link between the barn and the farmhouse, creating a dramatic double-height entrance hall, which flows through to a new kitchen to the rear while also connecting with a new staircase – welded to the back of the original stone building – leading to the upper floor.

These additions achieve a great deal. Not only do they provide new circulation routes, as well as a connector from the farmhouse to the barn, but they also bring a sense of drama and a grander sense of scale to the original buildings. The sculptural, sinuous quality of the new elements marks them as contemporary, sitting in contrast with the linear nature of the original stone structures, but at the same time there is a degree of discretion, with the new interventions subservient in height and position to the period farm buildings.

The farmhouse itself was restored and updated, including a process of reorganisation within. The ground floor features a study/library that flows into the main drawing room, now occupying a significant portion of the plan. The floor above is taken up by the master suite – a triptych of layered spaces, with the bedroom at one end, the bathroom at the other and a dressing room in between.

A project of many parts and multiple dimensions, Watergate can be compared to the invention of modern farmsteads, such as Hannington Farm and Fulford Farm. Yet here in Oxfordshire the challenges were, in some ways, more complex, involving a mixture of new interventions, reinventions and master planning aimed at bringing all of these elements together in one cohesive, ordered home.

Pages 108–109
From the car porch to the staff cottage.

Right
The rebuilt barn, now an artist's studio with a lime floor and lime insulation to the walls, along with a single towering sheet of glass.

Opposite
The studio barn showing the giant top hung external shutters.

Reinventions and Adaptations: Watergate

Left
The new link of oak, lead and concrete between the barn and the original farmhouse.

Opposite
The curved cladding to the new staircase.

Opposite, far right
From the new first floor landing down to the entrance hall.

Reinventions and Adaptations: Watergate

The Timeless Home

Left
The staff cottage.

Above
The main approach to the farmstead, with glimpses of the car porch, the entry gate to the courtyard and the staff cottage between them.

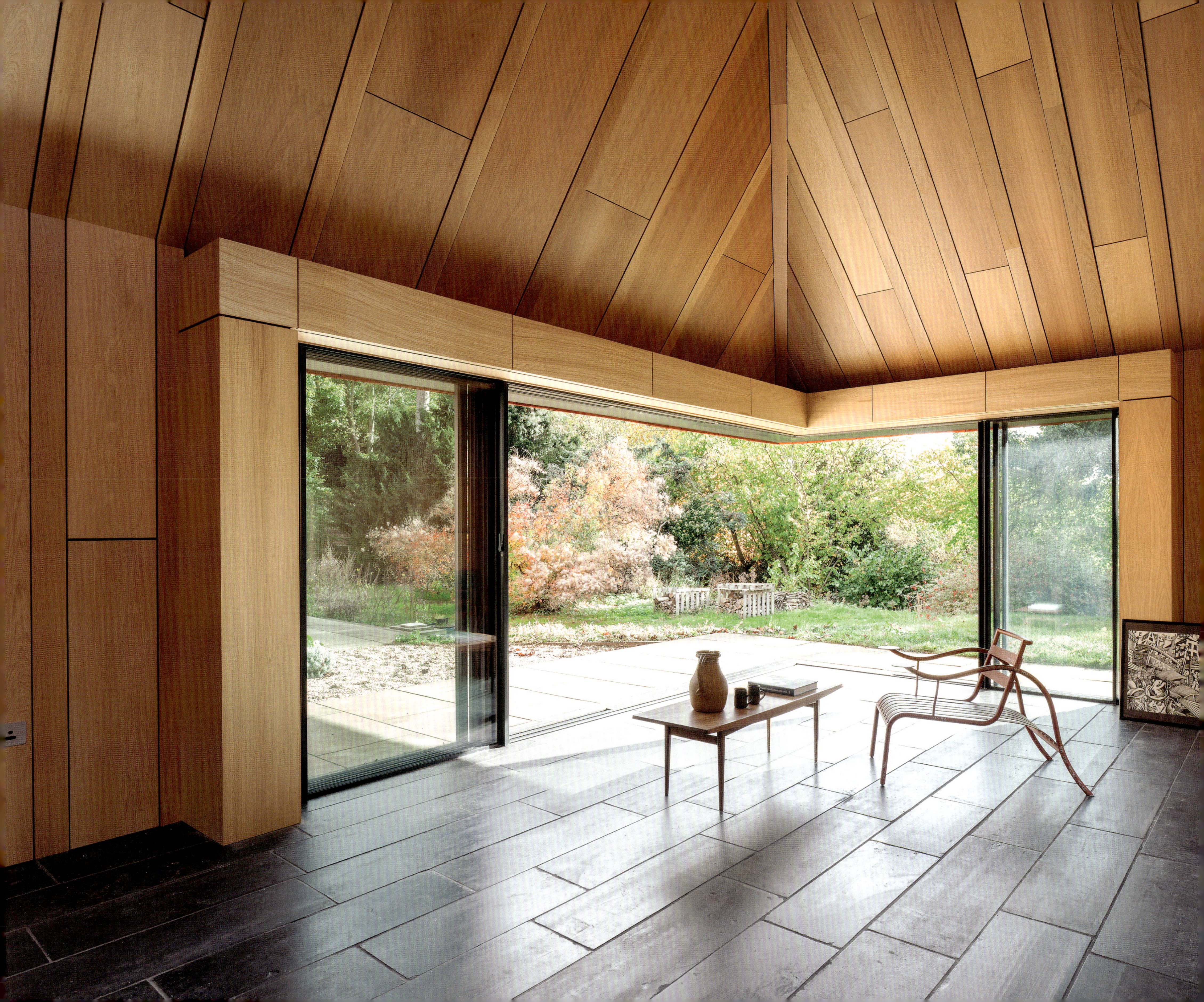

Downs House

Suffolk
2016

One of the great delights of English rural homes, such as Downs House, is the way that they have evolved over time. The original portion of the two-storey farmhouse dates back to the 15th century, which was extended in the 16th and again in the 18th. In this respect, James Gorst's new addition is the latest in a long line of adaptations and amendments.

The house itself is located in the picturesque village of Stoke-by-Nayland, north of Colchester. The 15th-century tower of St Mary's Church can be seen in the distance and was painted, many times over, by John Constable. The flamboyant 20th-century designer David Hicks also had a home here for many years, known as the Temple.

The owners of Downs House wished to extend the property once again with the principal aim of creating a studio, suitable for both work and pleasure. The clients were, initially, thinking of a glass box that could be grafted on to the run of period buildings.

'I felt that would be the wrong way to go and suggested that we design an echo of the original house instead', says Gorst. 'At the same time I thought it would be wonderful to place the echo almost opposite the farmhouse and so create a U-shaped plan, with the older additions in the middle. By doing so we would invent a semi-sheltered courtyard at the centre – an outdoor space that they would feel comfortable in, enjoying the gardens and the view.

At the same time, we wanted to come up with a form for the new section that was sympathetic to the very steep pitches of the roof of the Tudor house. The roof is in traditional clay peg tiles so we thought let's work with these traditional materials – the clay tiles – and the steep pitches and do something new but contextual.'

The original house also features tall, towering chimneys. These influenced the sculptural form of Gorst's addition, which features a semi-conical roof, like a funnel. The overall impression is of a building – and its pitched roof – cut in half, so that it forms a bookend on the site with a flat, straight back. The clay tiles coat the entire structure, reinforcing the sculptural quality of the addition, while a transparent glass link to the rest of the house creates a clear transition, or pause, between old and new.

Within, the semi-vaulted ceiling is a key feature. The walls and ceiling are coated in cubist panels of veneered oak ply, while the floors are in reclaimed slate. A corner window slides back on two elevations to create an open relationship with the courtyard alongside. The client has mounted an art collection upon the walls of the studio – which is top lit by a skylight – reinforcing the impression of a gallery space.

'There is this sculptural delight in volume and height with this building', says Gorst. 'It's about the desire to break out of the normal constraints of domestic architecture and dabble in pure form. But there's also a lot of craft to it, as well as these traditional materials. You can achieve a lot in terms of breaking new ground with a building when you work in materials that people do find reassuring and familiar.'

In this way, and others, the addition is highly contextual as well as abstract. Beyond the studio itself Gorst rebuilt a piggery alongside to serve as a games room, while the 18th-century portion was also altered and updated. Here, a mezzanine was removed to create another open, generously proportioned space, which now serves as a library, bordered by bespoke bookcases. A long dining table to the centre means that the library can serve not only as a reading room, but also offer a space for entertaining.

As with Watergate, Downs House is not only about new additions but also about looking at the bigger picture. New meets old, offering fresh juxtapositions and contrasts, but existing spaces and their function are also re-examined within the master plan. The practice's interventions add another chapter to a complex and fascinating narrative that has developed over many centuries.

Pages 116–117
Downs House looking out to the garden and down the hill to Nayland beyond.

Below
The new library.

Opposite
Inspired by the steep-pitched clay peg tiled roof of the original Downs House. Constable's Stoke-by-Nayland church tower is in the distance.

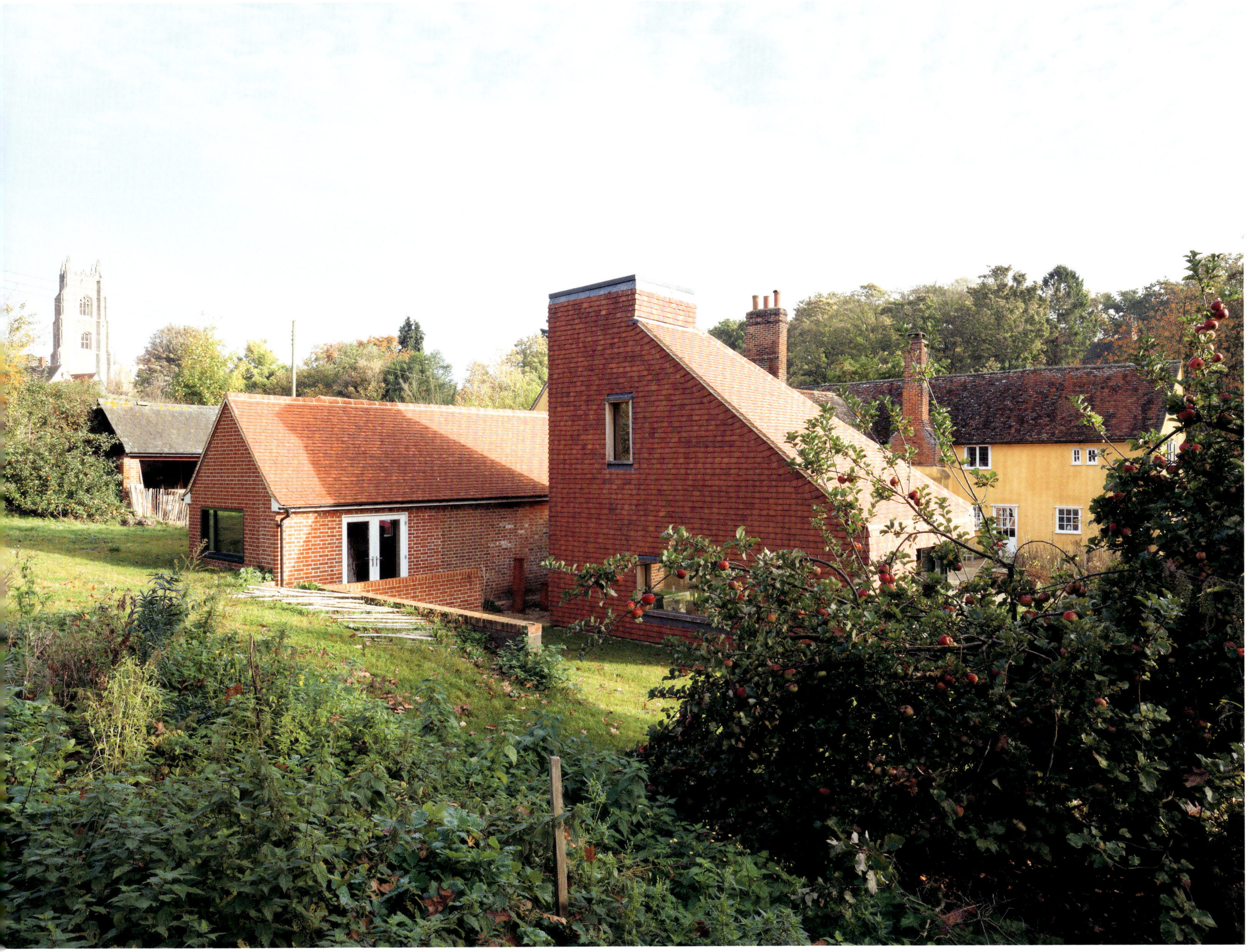

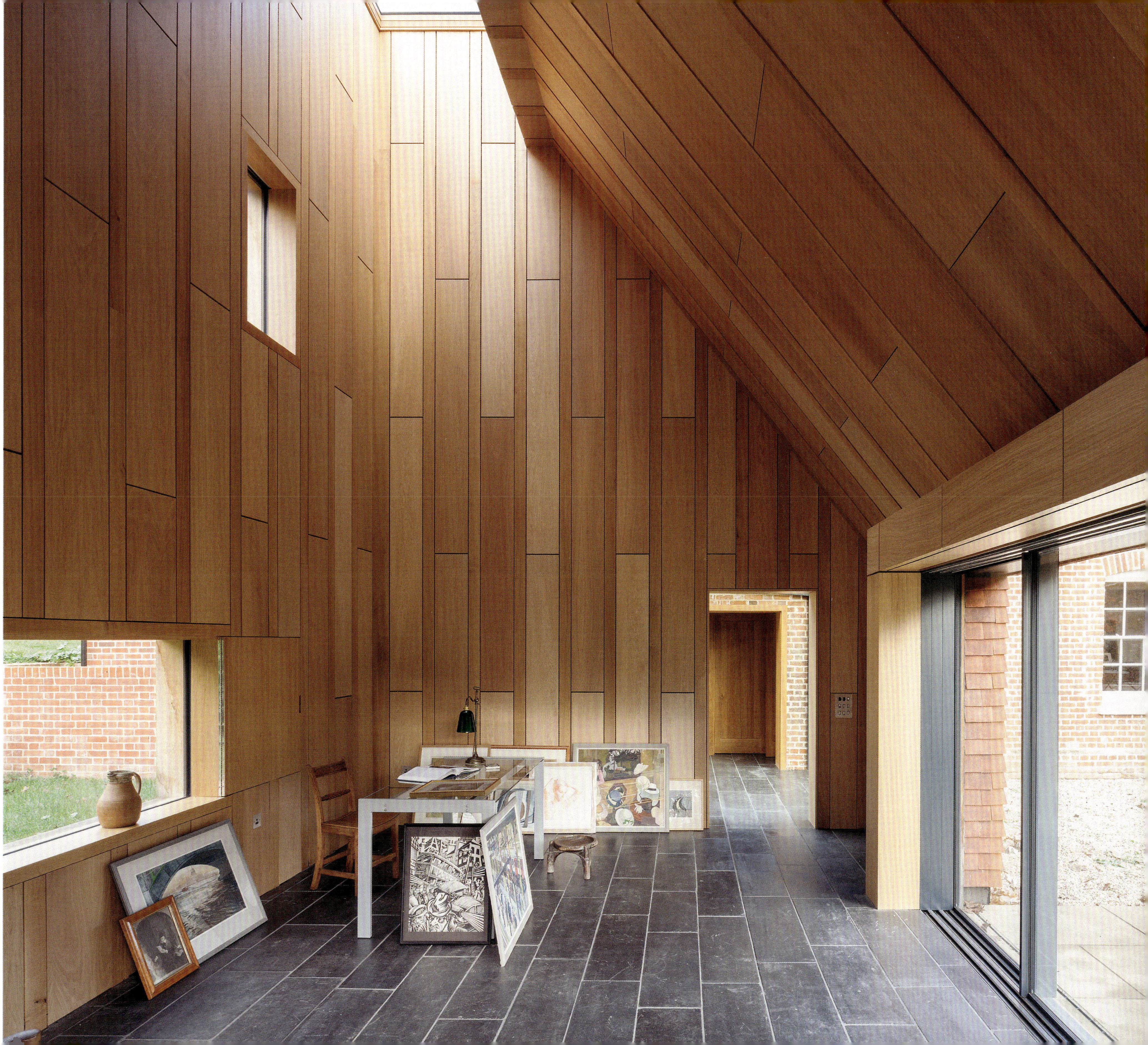

Left
The gallery before the hang – the panelled walls are now a mosaic of paintings.

Right
Converging perspectives and fastidious joinery.

Left
'A contextual piece unshackled by functional imperatives' an essay in form, volume and material.

Opposite
The plan shows how the new extension creates the amenity and intimacy of a courtyard garden in which to sit and eat and socialise.

Reinventions and Adaptations: Downs House

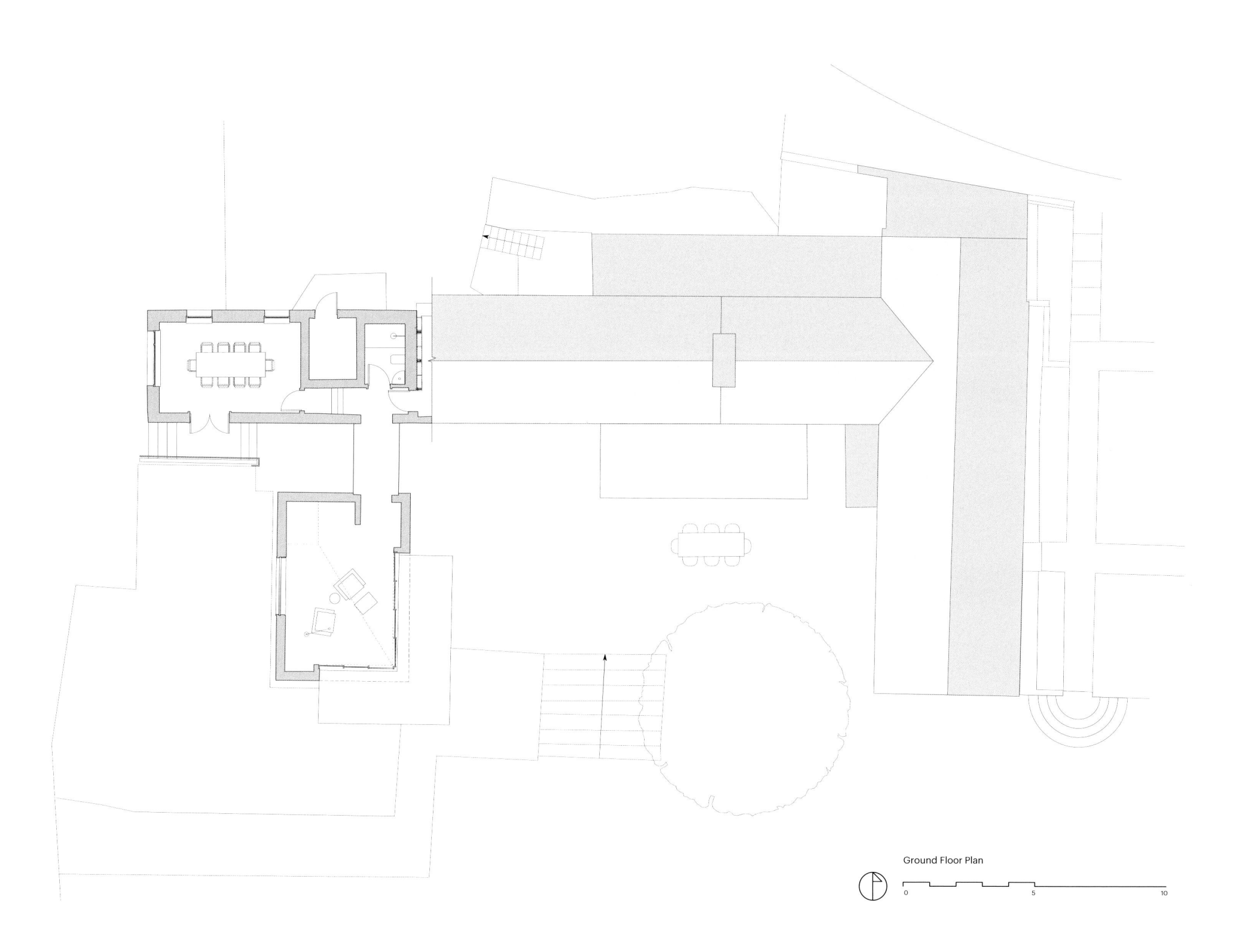

Ground Floor Plan

0　　　　　5　　　　　10

123

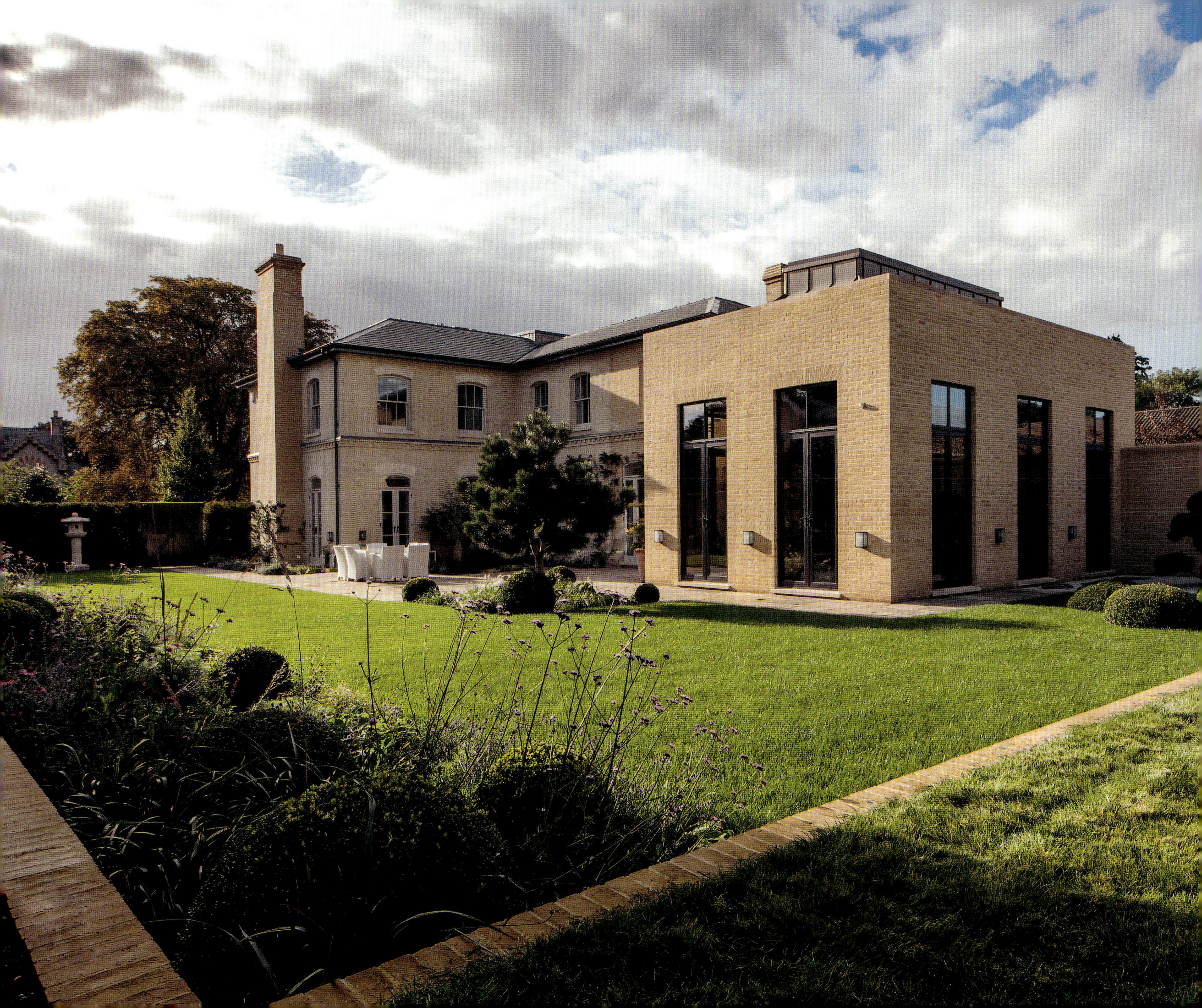

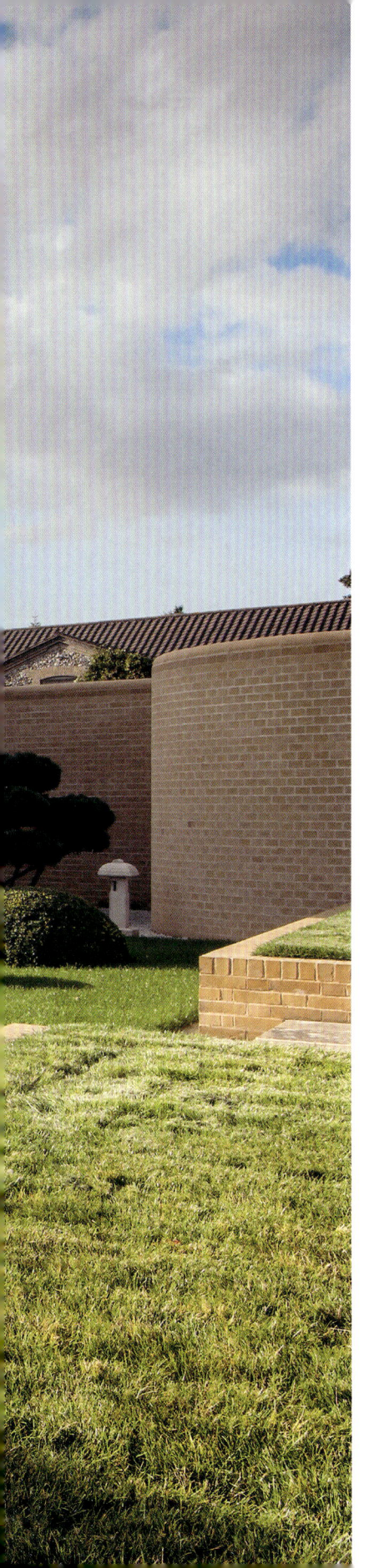

Hurworth House

Suffolk

2014

The Suffolk town of Newmarket is famous for its growing population of thoroughbred racehorses. For centuries it has been a focal point for horse breeding and racing, with over 50 horse-training stables now in and around the town. Much of the heritage of Newmarket is defined by its links to horse racing and the same could be said of the local economy.

James Gorst was approached by a private client with ties to this world and a passion for horse racing. He had acquired a Victorian house in the town, sitting within a substantial walled garden and with stables nearby. The original brick building dates from the 1850s and had been compromised by a series of extensions dating from the 1960s. The client wanted not only to extend the house but to bring order and clarity to the residence as a whole.

'It had become a maze of corridors, dead ends and right-angle turns', says Gorst. 'What was interesting about this project was that we needed to totally retell the story of the plan and the way that you move through the house. We always try to have this idea of spaces opening out and offering one surprise after another, while creating a rational circulation route, and that was especially important here.'

A significant portion of the original floor plan of the ground floor was essentially wasted space, with multiple hallways, passages and underused cellular rooms. Gorst's solution was radical, sweeping away all of these partitioned and muddled spaces to create an entirely new sequence of interrelated spaces, as well as replacing the old extensions with a modern addition, also in brick.

The reinvented ground floor offers a new floor plan, including a repositioned entrance hall and stairway, introducing a fresh sense of order. From here, one steps into family living spaces to either side and through into a spacious, open-plan kitchen and dining area, which effectively becomes the hub of the house. This, in turn, leads through to the new part of the building – a contemporary version of the 'great room' or 'great hall', offering an open and flexible living space with high ceiling and a series of tall French windows looking out onto the freshly landscaped gardens.

'I wanted the extension to have a dramatic presence of its own', says Gorst, 'and by building it in the same Cambridge brick as the original house it becomes contextually responsive. It's a rationalist piece that doesn't detract from the main building and has its own character, but they are joined together by materiality. It has become a fabulous new room, with these windows on three sides.'

This new space has the feel of a library, top lit by a long central skylight, and lined with wall and ceiling panels in walnut,

The Timeless Home

Pages 124–125
The new garden elevation.

Left
The library.

Right
The library roof in French-polished English walnut.

which has been French polished. Bookcases are integrated among the wall panels and the door frames are in bronze. The interiors throughout are characterised by thoughtful restraint, with an emphasis on rich, crafted and characterful materials. The same can be said of the drawing room, which – along with the rest of the house – was stripped back and recreated, with a new fireplace and a panelled plaster ceiling, created with a restrained geometry.

'It was a question of thinking about what would be appropriate for the interiors, which are no longer early Victorian', says Gorst. 'It's more august, sober but sophisticated with something of a pared-down Deco quality to the mouldings, doors and details. There's a touch of Emile-Jacques Ruhlmann but also a degree of stripped-down classicism, with a good deal of subtlety and a sense of calm.'

Upstairs also saw a complete reworking, with the creation of four spacious, en-suite bedrooms as part of a new layout that sits within the outline of the original building. In a way, the project represents the creation of a new house – with a fresh floor plan – inside the Victorian shell. The original building offers a context that has been treated with respect, while also seeking to fashion a contemporary and more informal way of living throughout.

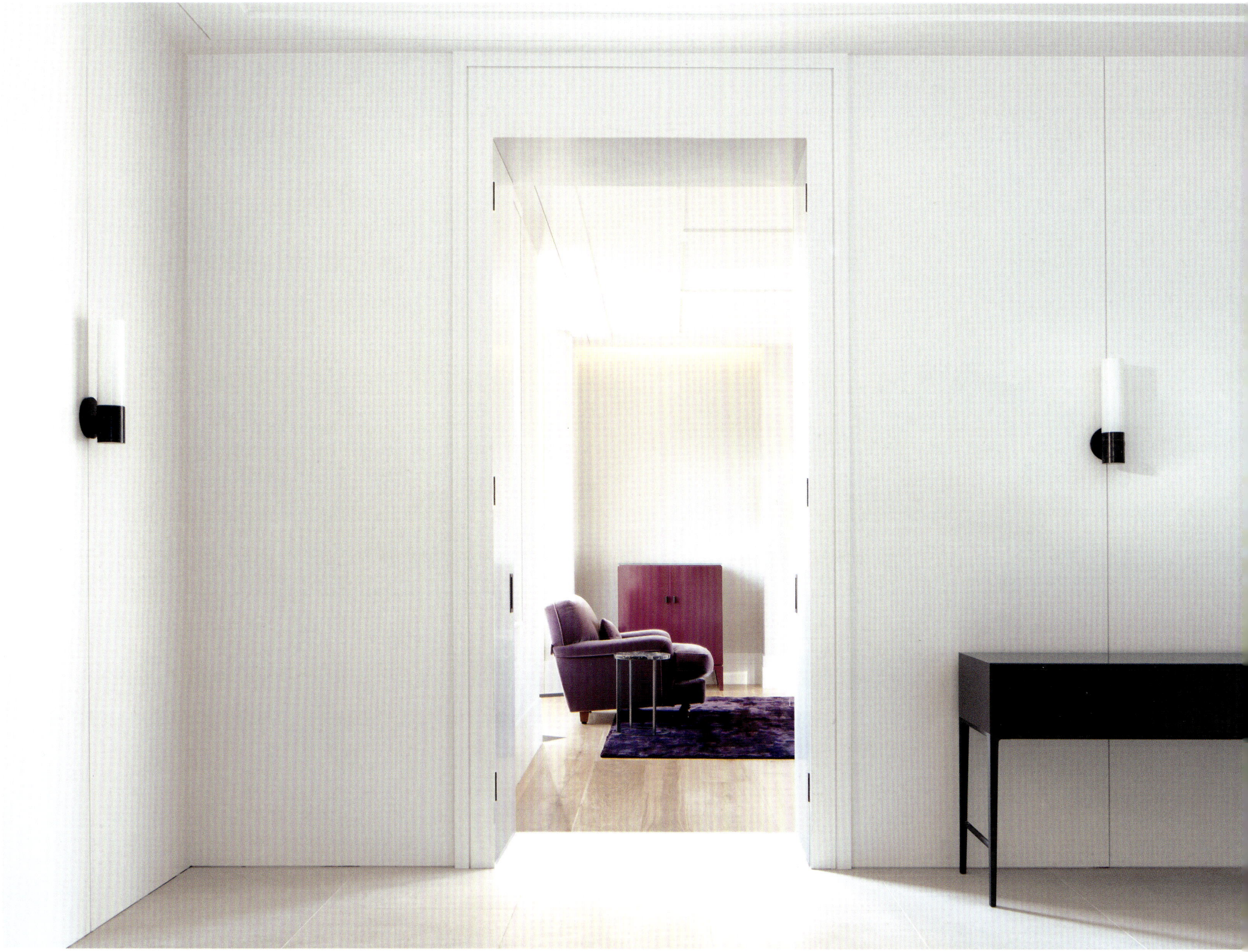

Opposite
From the new panelled entrance hall to the Morning Room. Sconces by Remain Lights, Brooklyn.

Right
The new hall and stair.

Above
The stables elevation –
Cambridge gault bricks and
knapped flint.

Below
The ground floor plan of the remodelled house.

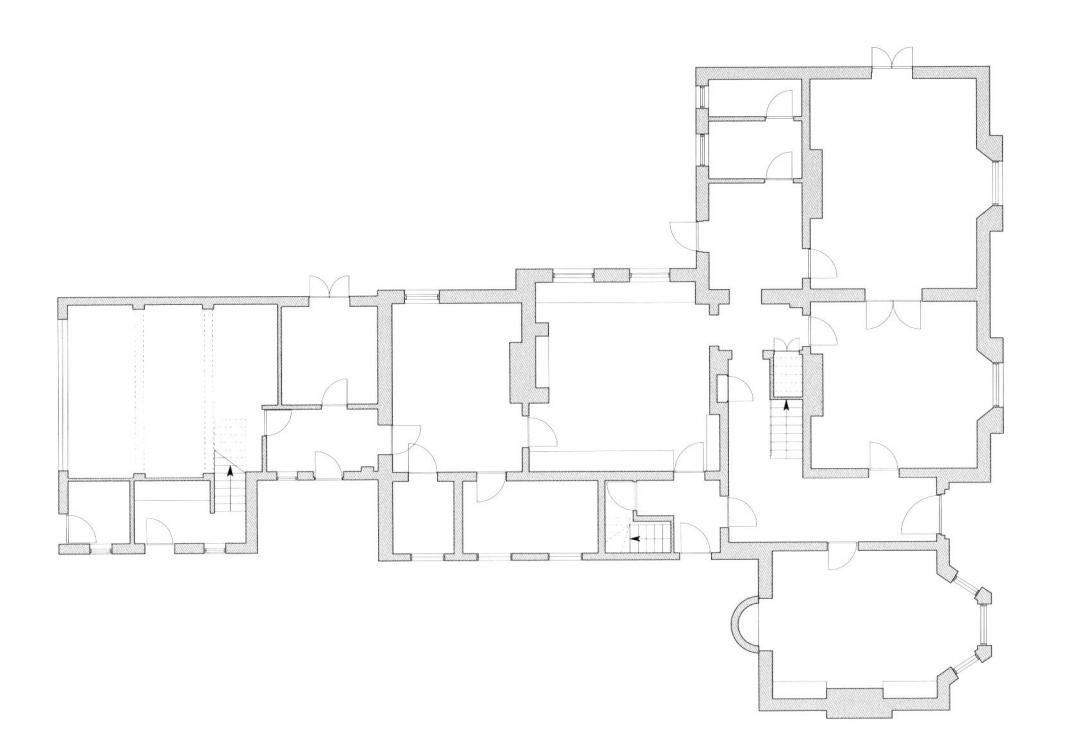

Existing Ground Floor Plan

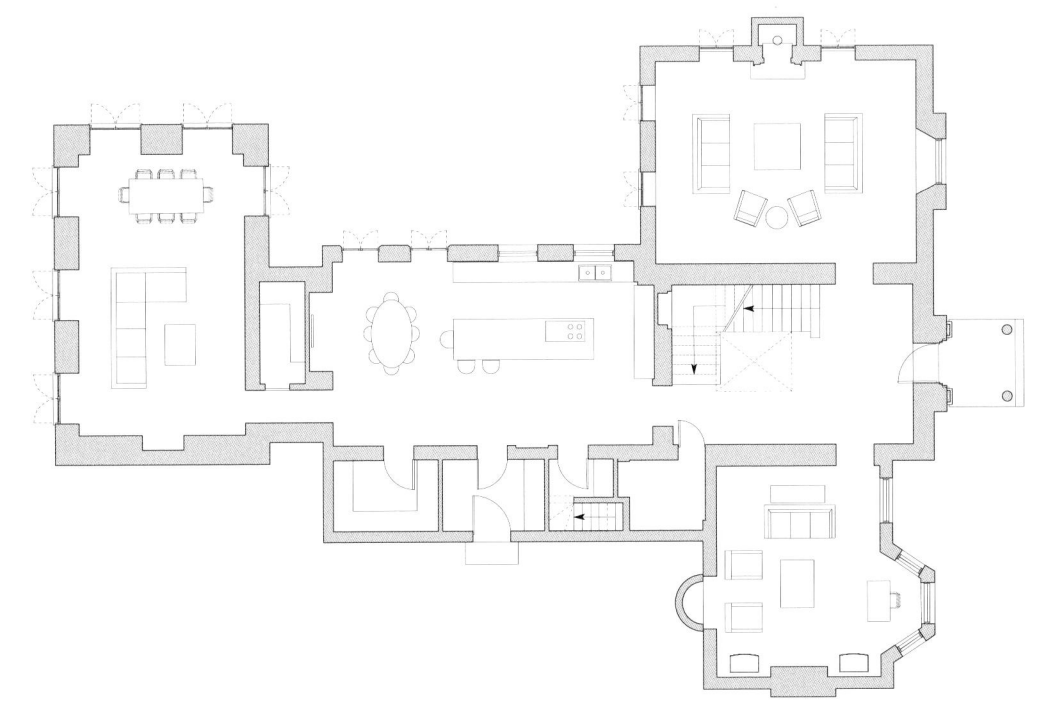

Proposed Ground Floor Plan

Reinventions and Adaptations: Hurworth House

131

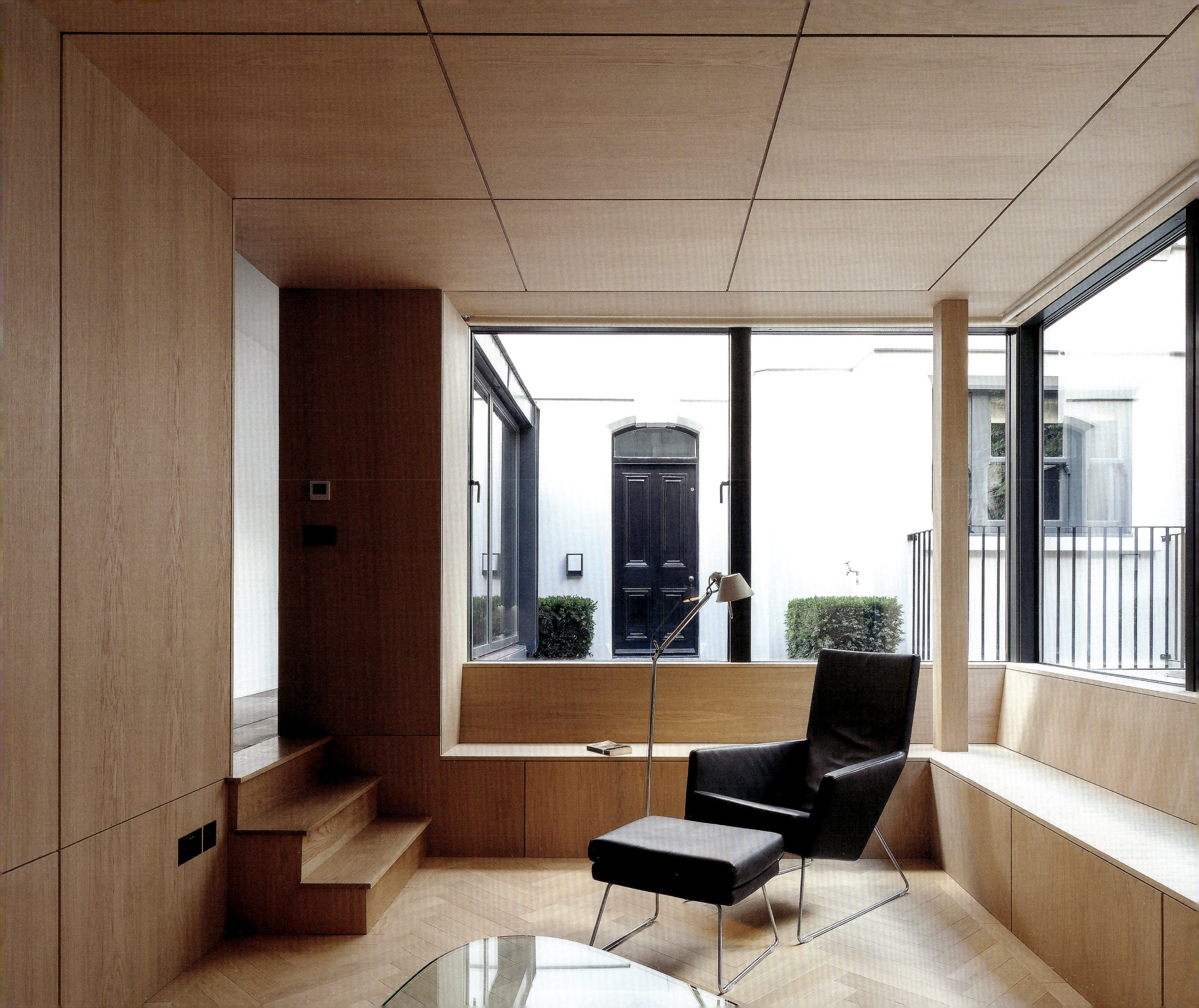

House of Detention

London
2016

The House of Detention, in a quiet quarter of Clerkenwell, is a highly personal project for James Gorst. For around 17 productive years this charming period building served as the offices for Gorst's architectural practice. But recently Gorst decided to move the London office, while also spending more time living and working in Suffolk. This created an opportunity to update and extend the building, which has been transformed into an enticing family home.

The original 18th-century building served as a prison governor's house, sitting alongside the Clerkenwell House of Detention. This was a remand prison, built around 1820 on the site of two earlier and older prisons. The building found fame – or notoriety – as the scene of the 'Clerkenwell Outrage', which saw an explosion aimed at freeing an arms supplier to the Fenians, Richard Burke; 12 died in the blast.

The main prison building was demolished around 1890 but the governor's house remained, along with a series of vaults below ground. A school was then built on the site, which was – in turn – converted into apartments. The governor's former home was, briefly, part of a museum and was then put on the market in the year 2000, when Gorst bought the property.

'What drew me to the House of Detention was that it was this incredibly private world, hidden away behind the old prison walls', says Gorst. 'Nobody knew what was there because it was so hidden away. You step through a door in these high walls and you are in a secret courtyard garden and find this delightful house.

I have always disliked traditional offices and the subjugation of people to office life, so I loved the idea of being in this house with a garden, a fish pond and a pergola. It offered us such a welcoming place to work, rather like a home for us all, but in this very central London setting.'

Following the recent relocation of the offices, Gorst embarked on the restoration of the original building, as well as the design and build of a two-storey addition within one part of the courtyard garden. Through a process of remodelling and extending, Gorst was able to double the available living space and create a four-bedroom house with two sitting rooms.

'I was very interested in the counterpoint between the period house and the contemporary extension', Gorst says.

'We went above and beyond in terms of renovating and updating the original house, which actually dates back to around 1740. We reintroduced the fireplaces and brought in mouldings, architraves, cornices and so forth, which has made it more rhetorical and grander than it might have been originally but fits with the aim of transforming the house into something more substantial overall.'

Pages 132–133
From the garden room to the House of Detention.

Left
The courtyard.

Opposite
A dynamic view of the corridor linking the House of Detention to the new courtyard pavilion. The transparency of the glazed corner shows the sunken floor of the pavilion sitting room. In the summer all the glazed screens open to extend the house into the courtyard.

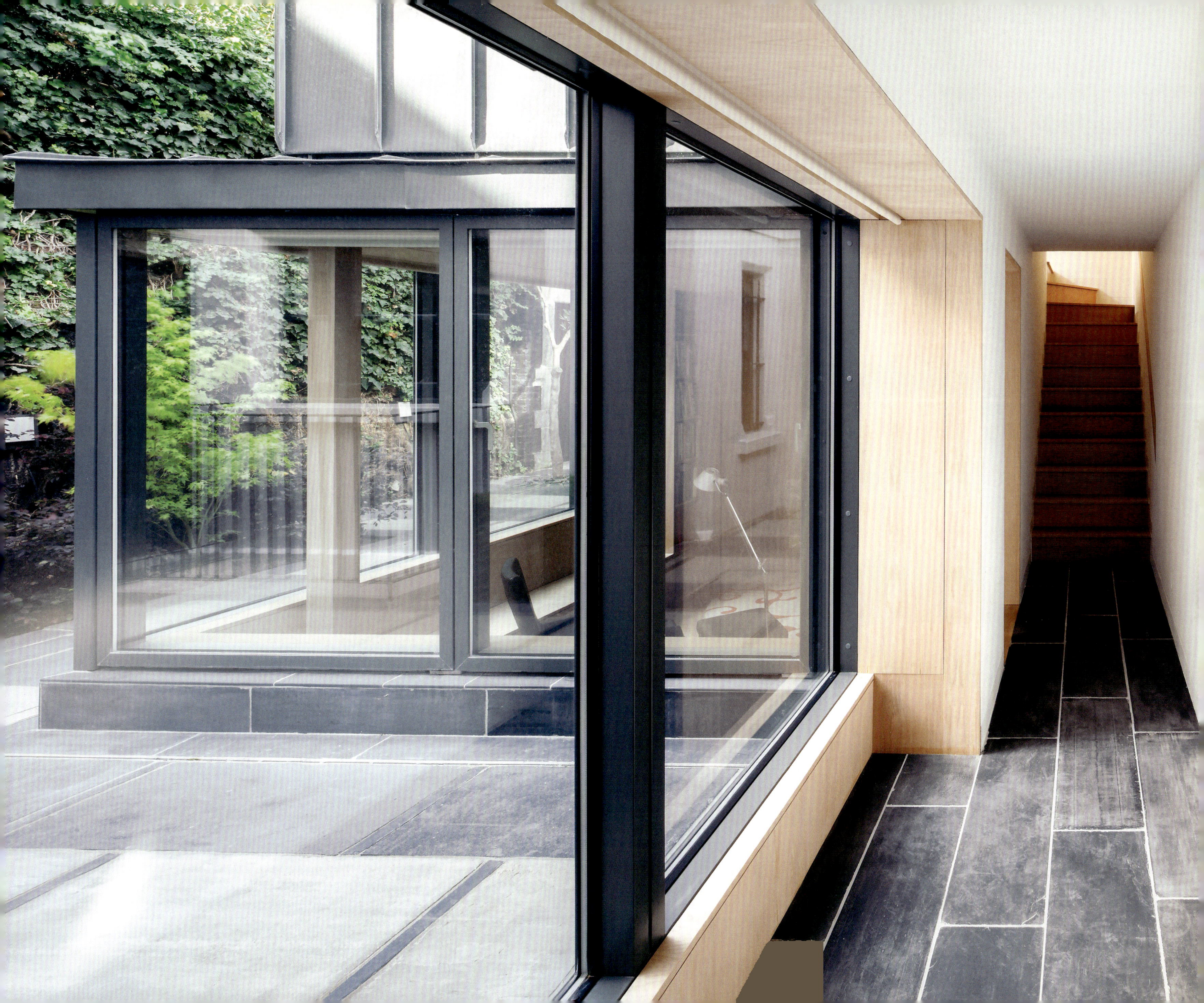

Far left
A sliver of book shelves in the panelled garden room.

Left
A panelled room in the old house.

Opposite
The garden room at dusk.

Gorst selected characterful materials of quality and provenance for both the reinvented period part of the house and the new addition, helping to tie them together. These include reclaimed slate flooring, used extensively on the ground level, yet also oak parquet. Wall panelling has been introduced extensively, with the period spaces featuring painted surfaces in a more traditional manner while the new addition features walls of veneered oak with joinery of a contemporary style.

The period house and the extension are clearly and respectfully distinguished from one another. A slim glazed corridor connects the two, while also framing an open view of the courtyard garden. The lower level of the addition holds a sunken drawing room with fitted window seats; here again there is a strong sense of connection to the secret world offered by the garden. Upstairs, in this new part of the house, Gorst designed a bedroom suite with a compact bathroom alongside and much in the way of integrated storage.

A key element of the success of the project is the dialogue between old and new, with the two portions of the building looking out at one another across the court, which is given privacy, security and seclusion by the high boundary walls. Like a Moroccan townhouse the combination of enclosure provided by the high, closed border and a hidden garden tucked within offers an endearing model.

'This idea of an enclosed world is certainly very comforting', says Gorst. 'It is a wonderful location for a home and it's almost silent here in the evenings and at night. It is this little private world sitting within this special quarter of Clerkenwell.'

Reinventions and Adaptations: House of Detention

Interiors
and Furniture

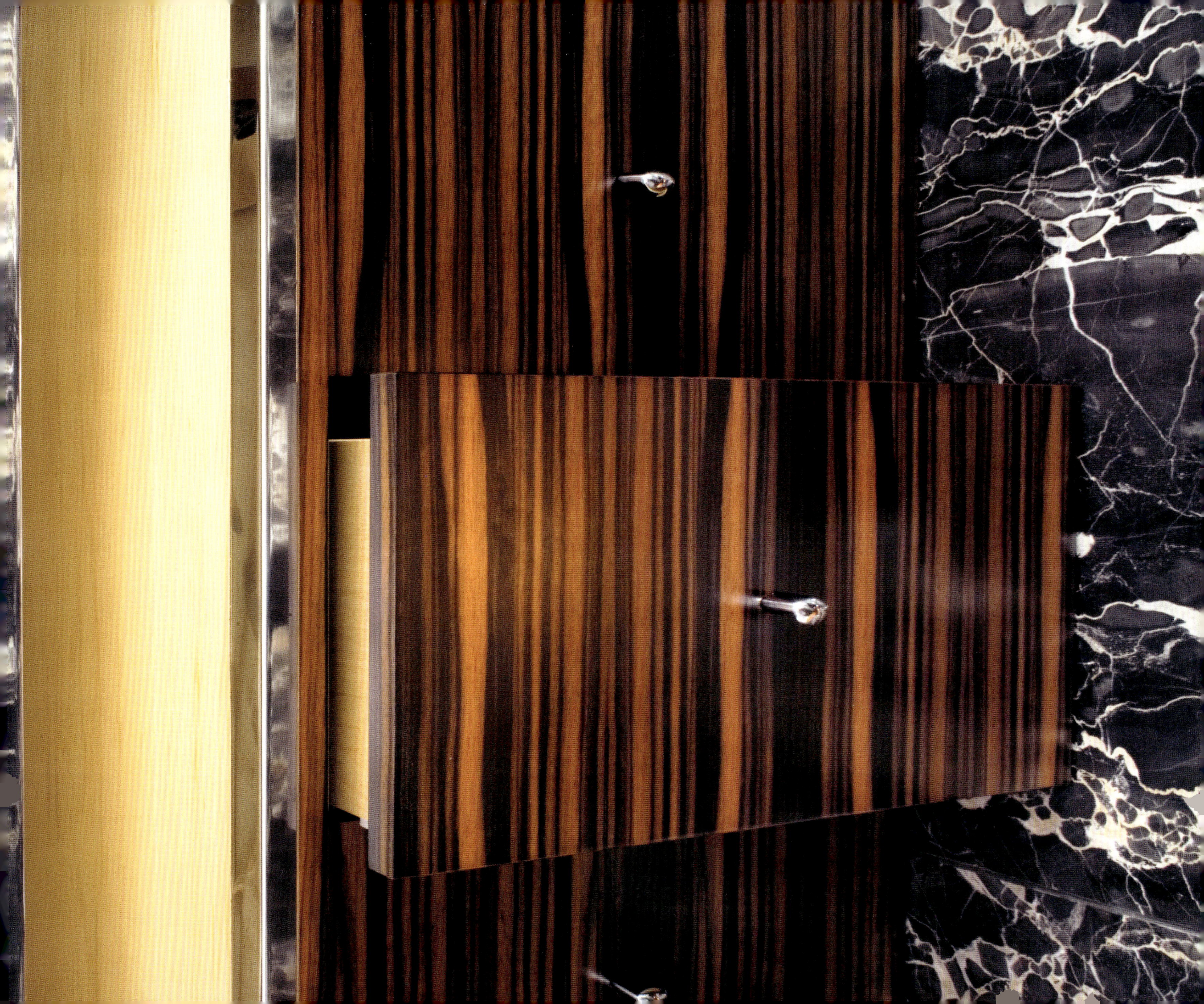

Interiors and Furniture

Along with many other contemporary architects, James Gorst has nursed – at times – a degree of suspicion about the role of interior designers. This does not imply a lack of willingness to collaborate, given that Gorst works closely with his colleagues, his clients and a spectrum of craftsmen, artisans, consultants and specialists of all kinds. It is more to do with the wish to maintain a degree of control over a design narrative and foster a sense of cohesion, rigour and unity that carries right through a project from beginning to end.

'As I worked on larger projects I realised the damage that could be caused by an unsympathetic interior decorator when the architect's work was considered incomplete', Gorst wrote in an October 2010 essay for the *RIBA Journal*. 'I realised that I needed to head them off and take on their role.'

Taking the example of Arts and Crafts masters such as Charles Voysey and Edwin Lutyens, or modernist pioneers such as Alvar Aalto and Frank Lloyd Wright, Gorst began to see architecture and interior design as two sides of the same coin. With the support and encouragement of key clients – some of whom commissioned multiple projects – Gorst began to embrace a totality of design. Rather than passing on his narrative, half-finished, to someone else, he and his colleagues were able to continue and provide the story with a beginning, middle and end.

For new-build homes, projects increasingly encompassed everything from planning to completion, from foundations to furniture and furnishings. The same can be said of adaptations and extensions, which also involved the provision of many bespoke elements from wardrobes, to headboards, to window seats, to kitchens and home libraries (a particular favourite for Gorst himself) with their layers of shelves populated and punctuated by knowledge and stories.

At the same time, in parallel, Gorst found himself being invited to take on more projects – particularly in London – that could be described as interior architecture, including updates and restorations of period houses as well as apartments. One of the most formative of these apartment commissions was Shelley Court, an apartment in an Edwardian mansion block in Chelsea. Here, Gorst was offered an almost blank canvas. The flat required not only a new layout and floor plan, but a fresh and original character.

Shelley Court, in particular, offered a sophisticated take on crafted modernism. The reference points were Adolf Loos, Eileen Gray and other pioneering modernists from the late 19th and early 20th centuries, along with touches of Emile-Jacques Ruhlmann and Jean-Michel Frank. These were designers operating along the borders of Art Deco and modernism itself, who loved both the beauty of fine, expressive materials and the possibilities offered by the machine age and the fresh push to linear abstraction and geometrical precision. Shelley Court, in its own way, referenced all of these things while creating a fully rounded space that was luxurious, crafted and masculine. The detailing was exquisite while the level of craftsmanship exhibited throughout was always striking.

Shelley Court led to other commissions that were more about interior design than architecture – apartments in Eaton Square, townhouses in Bloomsbury and Mayfair. Gorst would listen not just to his clients but to each building, taking his cues from the period and provenance of each one. Yet common threads included the increasingly bespoke nature of the spaces themselves, which were finely tailored according to form, function and aesthetics while making use of expressive materials. Banks of crafted storage helped to make these spaces cleaner and more practical, eliminating clutter and excess, but they also allowed the quality and finish of the materials room to breathe and be seen at their full height.

Pages 138–139
76 Eaton Square. A salute to Loosian high-style with Macassar, Nero Portero marble, satinwood, polished stainless steel and acid etched glass.

Such spaces connected the poetry and the prose.

Close collaborations with clients saw conversations about not only furniture, lighting, rugs and textiles, but also art. Paintings and sculpture became an integral part of the interiors themselves in certain cases, as at the two Eaton Square apartments for example, where they are key elements 'framed' by their surroundings on the one hand but also lending colour, texture and energy on the other.

As well as designing much in the way of integrated furniture, Gorst also began to create individual, standalone pieces. They first evolved out of a specific need for furniture that could not be found elsewhere or bought 'off the shelf'. A striking drinks cabinet at Shelley Court stands out in the mind, but there were also console tables, side tables, drinks tables and other designs that were born of particular projects, contexts and requirements, both functional and aesthetic.

Like the interiors designed by Gorst and his practice, the furniture collections explore a love of craft and a passion for beautiful, characterful materials, including bronze, leather and oak. Such pieces certainly involve creative collaboration, but the vital relationships are with artisans, joiners and metalworkers in Hertfordshire, Suffolk and Norfolk. Here, as with Gorst's work as whole, the attention to detail is all important. The results speak for themselves.

MALACHI MARTIN
Vatican
Hugh Walpole
OGILVY ON ADVERTISING
STATE OF EMERGENCY
HACKERS
STEVEN LEVY

Shelley Court

London
1995

There are times when a project demands a completely new narrative of design. Such a challenge arose with a request from a discerning client who asked James Gorst to remodel a nondescript one-bedroom apartment within an Edwardian mansion block in Chelsea. The existing flat was beset with problems, including wasted spaces and dead ends created by corridors and partitions, while the level of detailing was poor. A fresh start was required.

Around the time of the initial commission, in the mid 1990s, there was a fashionable preoccupation with white minimalism of a very pure kind. For both Gorst and his client, such an approach seemed entirely wrong for the apartment, which provoked a search for a richer, more engaging aesthetic in which a shared interest in fine, characterful materials and finishes could be fully explored.

'I have always been a big admirer of Adolf Loos and those turn of the century Viennese and European apartments', says Gorst. 'So I started thinking about stripping everything away and reworking the entire apartment with an influence from that period. Then Eileen Gray became the other important source of inspiration for the project, so we decided to have this combination of Loos, Gray and some more modern pieces. That translated into a quite a dark, sober, crafted backdrop with energy coming through from the furniture itself.'

Gorst created a new floor plan with an enfilade of interconnected rooms, avoiding any need for corridors or wasted space devoted solely to circulation. A palette of fine, expressive materials helps to tie these spaces together, while pared-back detailing allows the focus to remain upon the character and finish of the materials, as seen in the work of the proto-modernist Loos and the pioneering furniture and interiors designed by Gray. There are architraves in mahogany veneer around open doorways, herringbone floors in African hardwood, wall panelling in key areas and silk curtains throughout, creating a sense of quiet and timeless luxury.

'The narrative that we created carried us through and we were able to choose all sorts of interesting details like the door handles in pink bronze, or lamps with beautiful bronze and leather bases with velum shades', says Gorst. 'The colour scheme evolved from conversations with the client and two large abstract paintings by Sarah Raphael of the Australian outback that we chose for the apartment. The colours that we used on the walls of the living spaces then spun out from those paintings that you see in the dining room and the sitting room.'

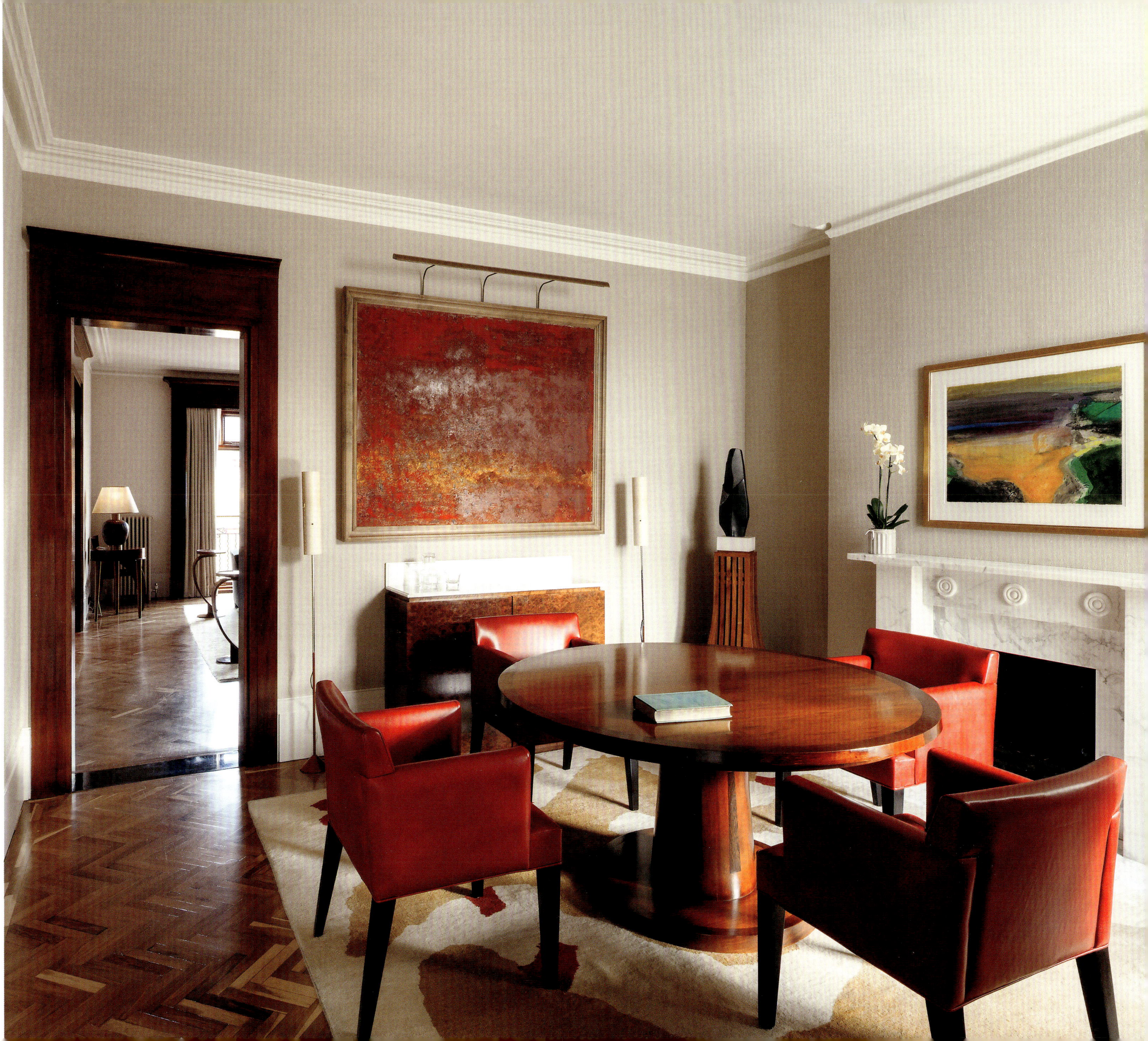

Pages 142–143
The mahogany library.

Opposite
The dining room with serge antique fabric walls, a Sarah Raphael painting of the Australian outback, chairs and table by Philippe Hurel.

Above
Curtained bedroom alcove.

Above right
The sitting room with Andrée Putman settees, a Sarah Raphael painting, drinks cabinet and flute tables by James Gorst.

Gorst was given a free hand over the entire project from beginning to end, lending the apartment a pleasing cohesion. This included selecting complementary furniture by Philippe Hurel and Andrée Putman, but also designing a number of bespoke pieces especially for the project (known as the Tite Street Collection). This marked the beginning of an openness to the idea of creating new collections of furniture generated by particular projects where there was a particular need to create pieces that would fulfil a precise function, yet also sit well within the context of the space in question.

'The first collection for Shelley Court grew out of this story we had created for the apartment and its spirit', says Gorst. 'Those pieces of furniture continued the narrative thread and were all about the materials, veneers, finishes and detailing. In a way this is what every architect wants to do, as you see not just with Loos and Gray but Charles Voysey and Edwin Lutyens. When you design a house or a room you want to design the furniture and pieces within it because it continues a line of thought.'

There are drinks tables and footstools, side tables and a chest of drawers. A standout piece is the multi-legged drinks cabinet in the sitting room, which looks as though it might scurry away. The craftsmanship of such pieces continues the exacting standards set elsewhere in the apartment, including the mahogany panelling in the library.

There is a relatively masculine character to such spaces, seen also in the bedroom and dressing room. Here, the precision of the joinery and the character of the veneer is reminiscent of a luxurious 1930s' train carriage. The bed is framed within an alcove and bordered by wraparound curtains, creating a more intimate scale and setting. Here, and elsewhere in this apartment, detail is everything.

Left
The entrance featuring Loosian mahogany veneers and Nero Portero marble.

Opposite
The dressing room towards the shower room with Pullman-style sapele pommele veneers.

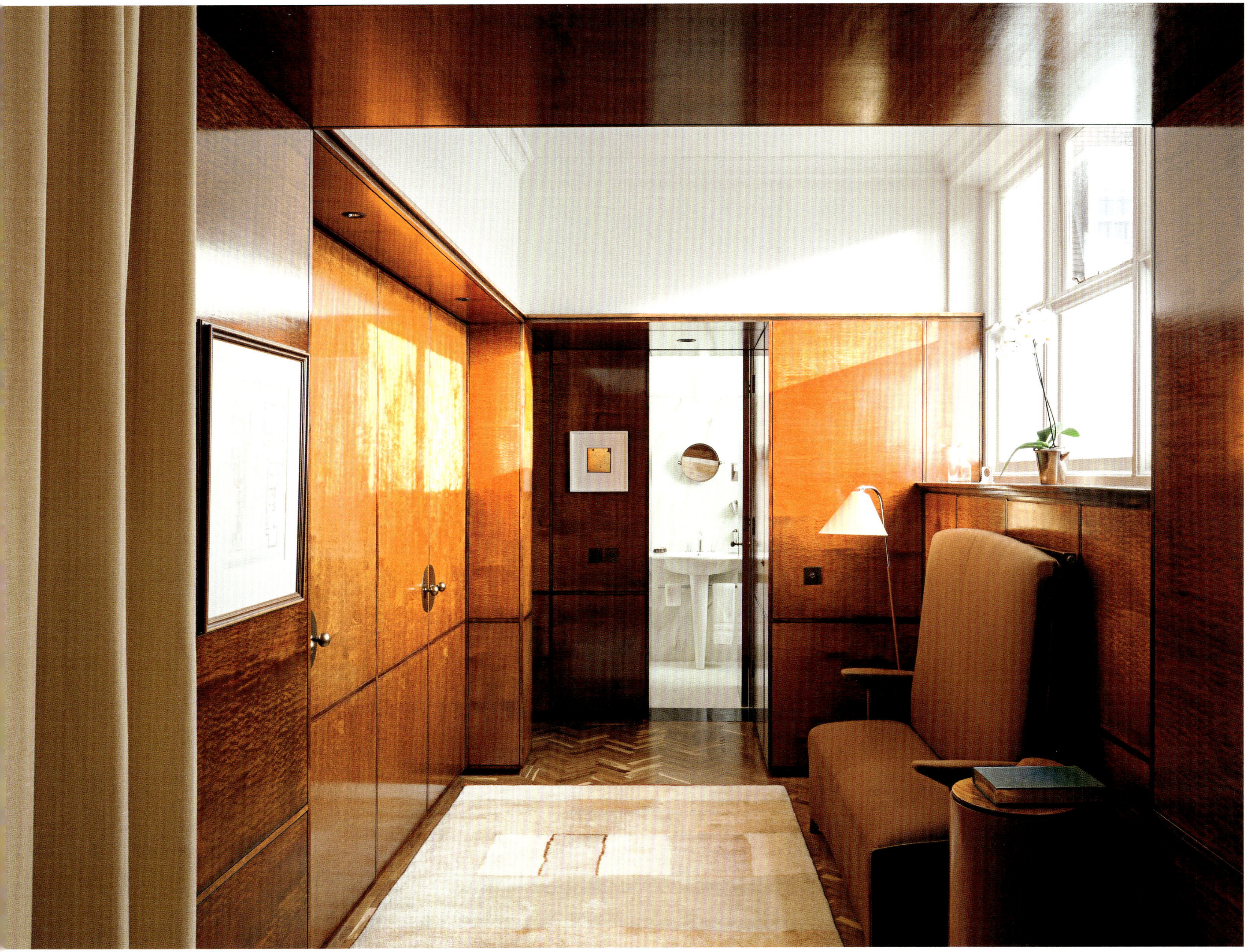

The Timeless Home

148

Opposite
A family of pieces in bronze and leather.

Right
A gathering of tables designed for the occasional flute of champagne.

Interiors and Furniture

149

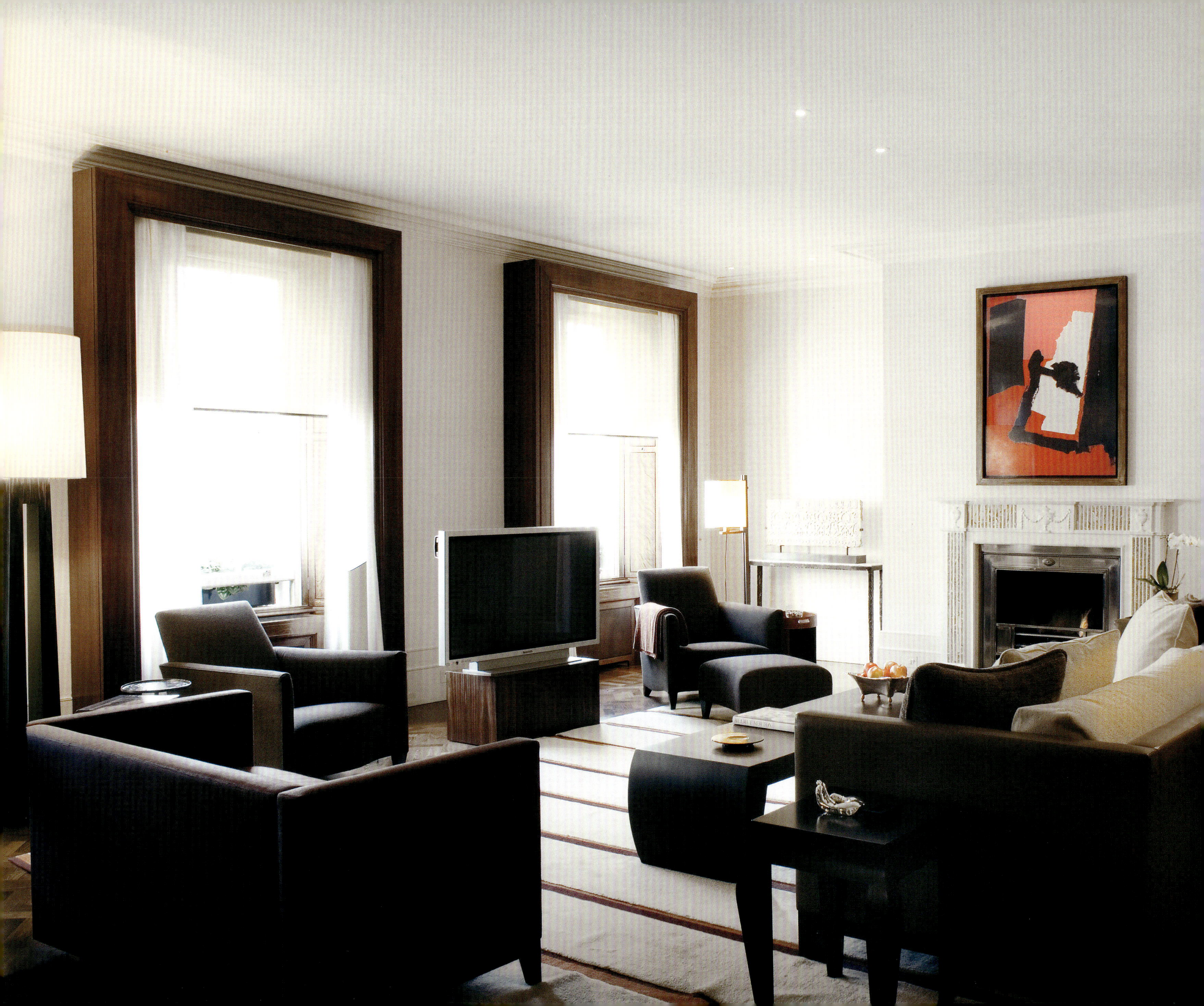

Eaton Square

Apartment One
London
1998

The grand, neoclassical houses of Eaton Square were largely created and laid out by the master builder Thomas Cubitt during the 1820s. It was one of three garden squares in Belgravia commissioned by the Grosvenor Estate and became home to prime ministers (Neville Chamberlain and Stanley Baldwin), ambassadors, actors and musicians. Today, most of the houses are divided into apartments but these are – generally – substantial in scale and generous in proportion.

Following on from the success of Shelley Court (see page 143), James Gorst was approached by new clients who had seen the earlier project published in the pages of a magazine. They had acquired a lateral apartment on the second floor of a house in Eaton Square and wanted to completely remodel the flat throughout, within a comprehensive approach that embraced interior architecture, decoration, lighting, furniture and other details.

'They were wonderful clients who we worked with for many years across a number of projects', says Gorst. 'Here, we ripped out everything and started again. You can see a certain influence or continuation from Shelley Court with a degree of sobriety that is lightened up by contemporary pieces and art, combined with these fine, crafted materials and detailing.'

Parquet floors help to unify the principal spaces, while architraves frame open doorways and windows. The main sitting room offers a spacious centre point, with seating around the fireplace and space for a bridge table to one side, positioned by one of the windows for a view of the garden square.

Here, as in Shelley Court, there is a degree of inspiration drawn from the 1920s and 1930s, particularly the work of Jean-Michel Frank and Emile-Jacques Ruhlmann, who were so adept at fusing luxurious materials and fine finishes with clean, modern lines. In the sitting room there are silk curtains at the windows, furniture by Christian Liaigre and Philippe Hurel, rugs by Sandy Jones, as well as a painting by Robert Motherwell over the fireplace, which provides a colourful focal point that shines out against a palette of predominantly neutral and natural tones.

Gorst and his clients travelled together to Italy and France choosing key pieces for the interiors. Lighting was selected, in part, to accentuate the choice of art, as well as providing task, accent and ambient light. The careful consideration of lighting design, as in Gorst's other projects, also helps to enhance the subtle but significant variations in texture and tone across the palette of materials.

As well as the more 'public' face of the apartment, the project embraced the idea of creating a series of more private

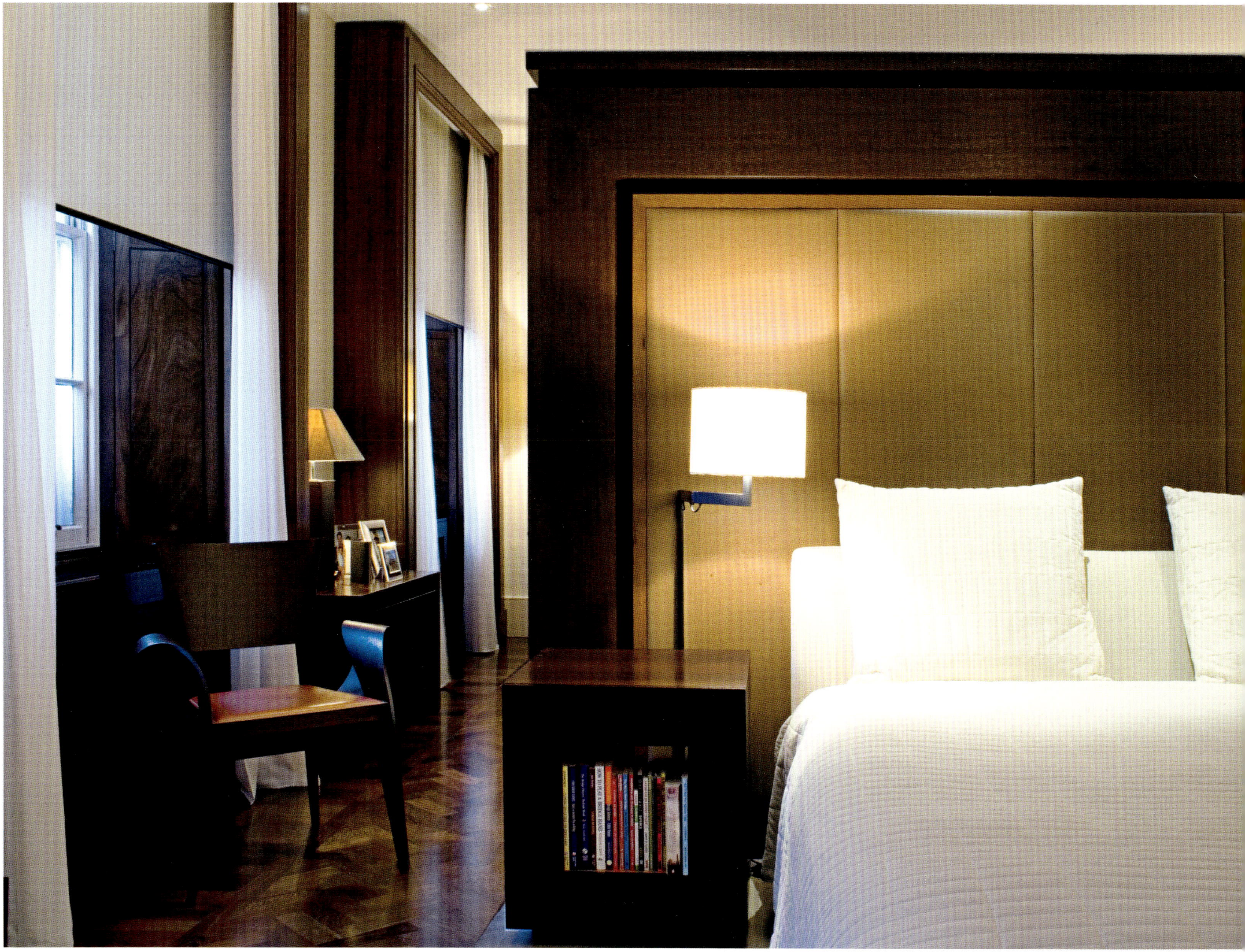

Page 150–151
The drawing room with furniture by Philippe Hurel and Christian Liaigre, rug by Sandy Jones and a painting by Robert Motherwell.

Left
Mahogany, iroko, leather and silk *'luxe, calme et volupte.'*

Right
Entrance hall with chairs by Sawaya & Moroni, sconces by Christian Liaigre and an abstract painting by Morris Lewis.

spaces of particular character and distinction. These include the master suite, where the bedroom sits alongside a dressing room and study, with bespoke storage tucked away in a partial partition between the two that doubles (on its opposite face) as a headboard for the bed.

The master bathroom is one of the most dramatic spaces in the apartment. Here, Gorst used Nero Portoro marble to great effect, creating a series of marble-clad enclosures for the shower and other services in a composition reminiscent of an art installation. The use of mahogany, glass and steel is also reminiscent of that transitional period of the 1920s and early 1930s where Art Deco morphed into early modernism. Integrated storage and drawers help to reduce clutter, reinforcing the visual impact of the materials themselves and the linear clarity of the space.

Left
The bathroom in wenge, Nero Portero, acid-etched glass, polished stainless steel and Macassar.

Right
A marble backed alcove containing a mirrored drug cabinet above a night time basin with a column of book matched Macassar drawers in the background, an architrave of Nero Portero marble and rat's tail veneered mahogany panelling to his and her private lavatories.

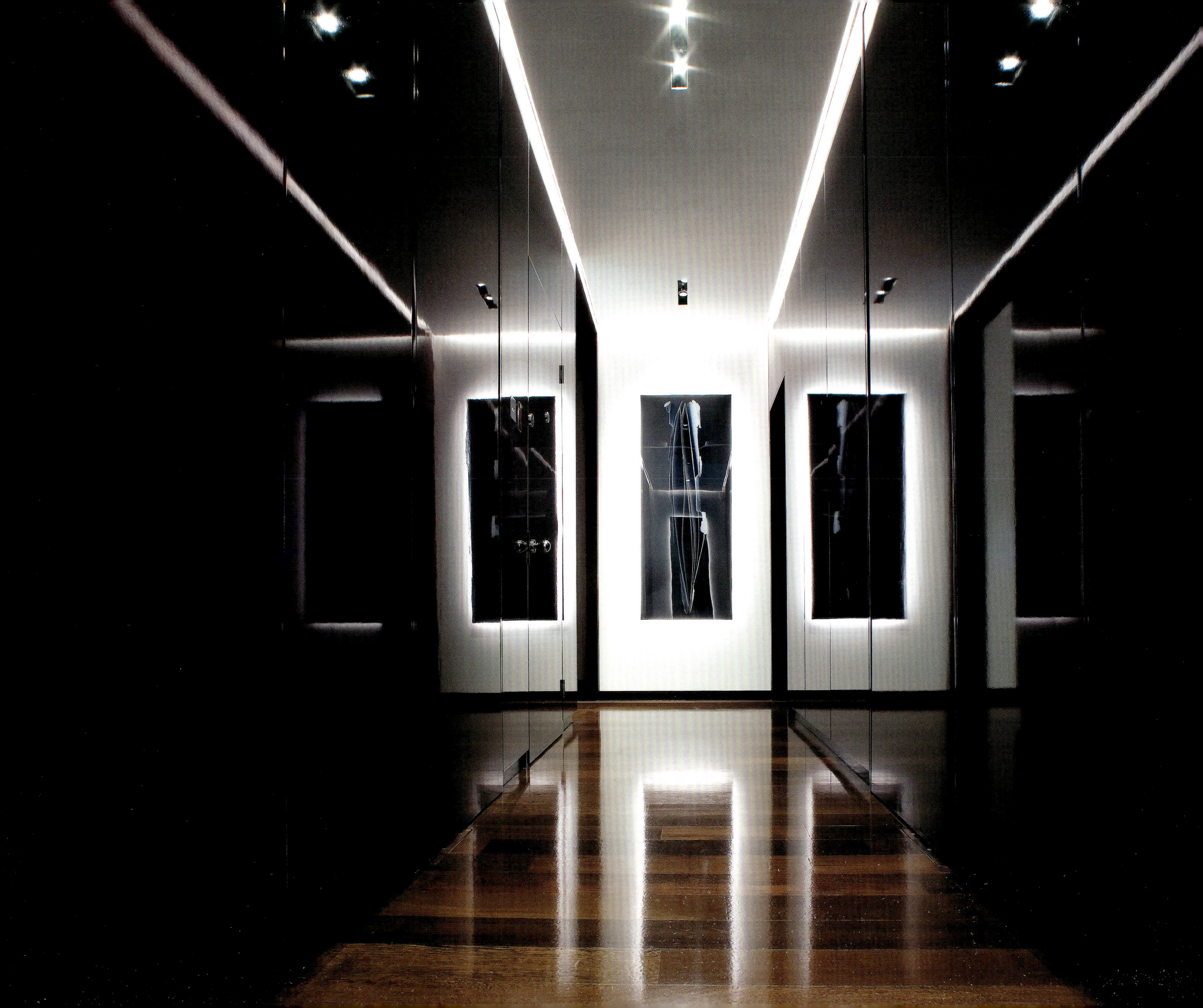

Eaton Square

Apartment Two
London
2004

Around three years after the completion of a commission for an apartment in Eaton Square in Belgravia, James Gorst was called back for a second project. Here, again, the context was a second-floor apartment in a Georgian house overlooking the garden square. Here, too, any internal period features – with the exception of the sash windows – had been lost over the years during a sequence of renovations and updates. Yet Gorst's approach was radically different this time around.

'I was excited about doing something slightly more contemporary and abstract', says Gorst. 'But what does connect them together – apart from the location – is the quality of the finishes and the sensuous character of the interiors.'

The clients – whom Gorst already knew well – wanted the living spaces to be light and inviting yet the entry sequence to the apartment, with limited natural light, made this a challenge. Gorst decided to explore a purposeful contrast between dark and light, creating more of a progressive promenade through the flat than a minimalist, all-neutral palette might provide.

'The entrance was always going to be quite dark because of its position within the building, which couldn't be changed as it's connected to a communal staircase', says Gorst. 'So we decided to make the hall as dark and enigmatic as possible so that when you emerge from it and step into the light you have that sense of surprise and an unfolding of space. We created these dark, highly lacquered surfaces for the walls and fitted cupboards in the hall where everything starts to dematerialise because of the reflections. The whole apartment is about blurring boundaries of different kinds.'

The practice selected a deep aubergine with a high-gloss finish for the banks of storage units and wall panels that line the hallway. As the flat begins to reveal itself, this wall of colour becomes a ribbon that carries through the internal surfaces of various parts of the apartment, transforming into a wall of hidden cupboards in the dining room and again in the master bedroom, where the wall of colour also frames integrated seating. The floors, too, are reflective, with a highly varnished wenge throughout much of the flat.

Beyond the colour ribbon, however, as one moves into the apartment and towards the lighter portions offered by the tall windows overlooking the garden square, the palette shifts to one of whites, creams and neutrals. This is true of the sitting room, for instance, where walls, curtains and the textured rug are all in shades of white. This allows art and the darker pieces of furniture – including the B&B Italia sofa and ottoman – to stand out more prominently, accentuating the line and form of each piece.

Pages 156–157
A dark and disconcertingly reflective entrance hall.

Left
From the dining room to the drawing room. The snake of high gloss aubergine panelling wraps around from one room to another as a dominant theme in an otherwise white, open-plan apartment.

Opposite
The drawing room.

The kitchen, too, is all in white while the dining room alongside sits at a crossroads between darkness and light. This theme of sensory playfulness is explored further in spaces such as the master bathroom – a hall of mirrors, with reflections upon reflections. The use of mirror glass to such an extent is reminiscent of the Deco period, yet the overall aesthetic is very contemporary.

Gorst and his team designed a number of pieces of furniture – both loose and integrated – especially for the apartment, known collectively as the Mayfair series. Once again, the provision of so much in the way of integrated elements such as wardrobes, cupboards, bookcases and shelving, allows the apartment to remain relatively simple in its lines and surfaces, lending the spaces a gallery feel that allows the clients' art collection to be seen to full effect.

Interiors and Furniture: Eaton Square

Left
The main bedroom.

Below left
An upholstered bench in the main bedroom.

Opposite
A bathroom fit for Narcissus.

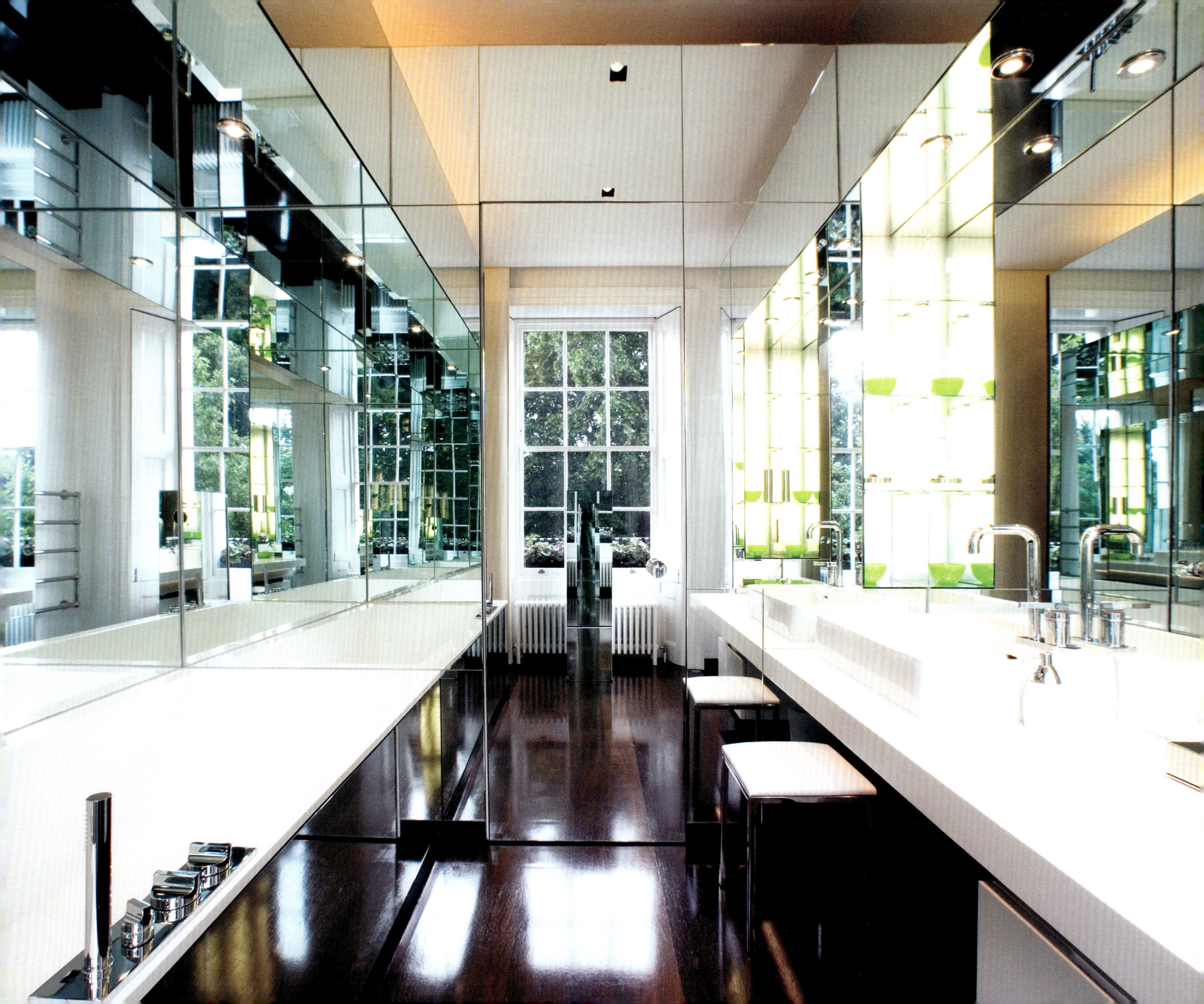

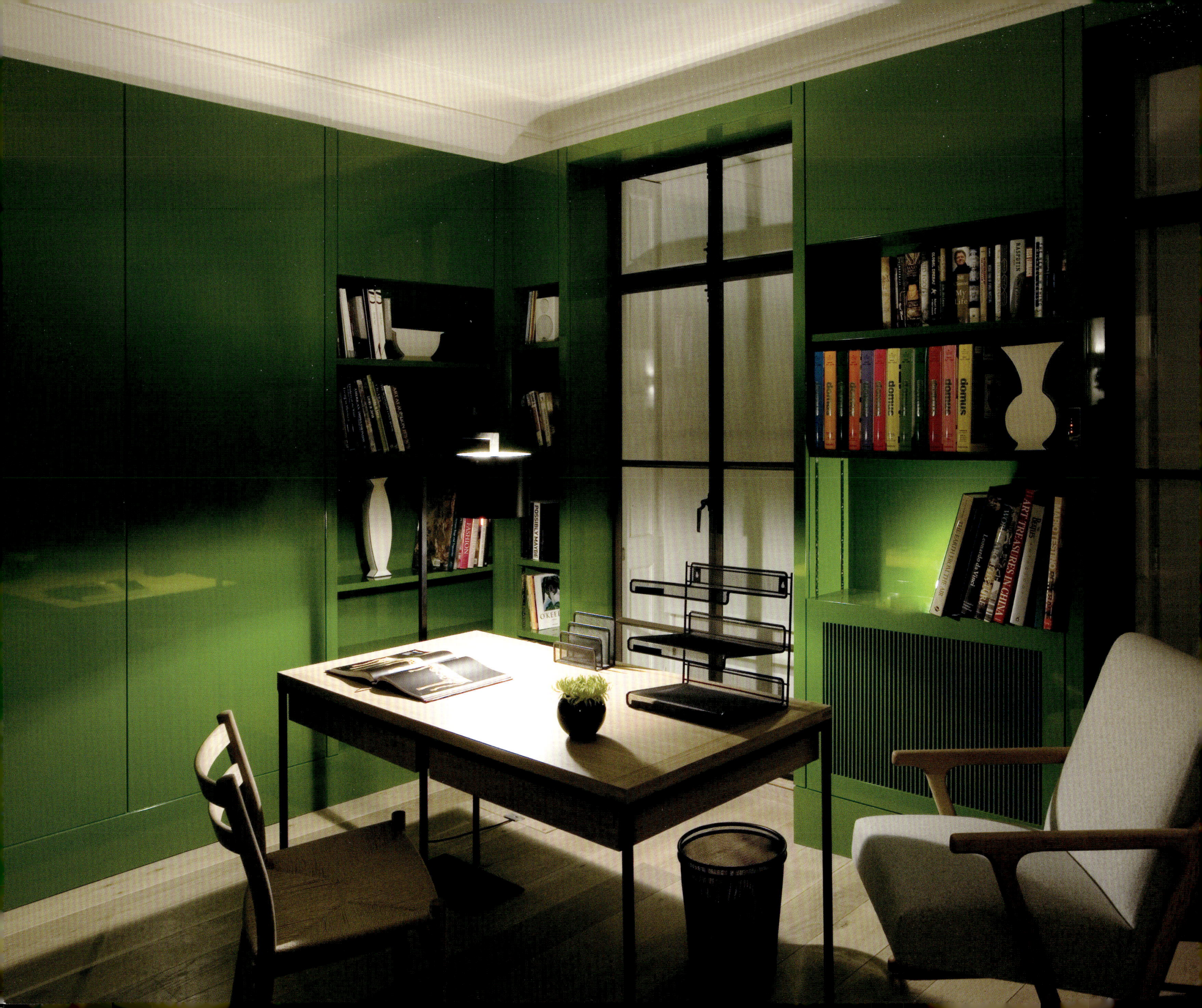

South Audley Street

London
2005

The period Georgian and Victorian houses of London and other major cities tend to be reinvented every 40 or 50 years. They adapt, often with admirable grace, to changing patterns of living and the more specific demands of individual owners and families. Each step in the evolution of such a period house becomes a balancing act that seeks to encompass past, present and future while creating a welcoming and practical home.

Over the years, James Gorst has grown familiar with such balancing acts. Given his understanding of both neoclassicism and modernism, he is more sensitive and respectful than most contemporary architects when it comes to the challenge of taking a period home into the 21st century. This was very much the case with this Georgian building in Mayfair, dating from the 1730s, which required reinvention with a light touch.

Gorst and his colleague David Roy were commissioned by repeat clients, who had already worked with the practice on two other projects. The six-storey house required restoration and revival, taking into account the vertical nature of this slim but well-proportioned building. With the notable exception of the staircase, many original features had been lost over the centuries, but the proportions of the spaces within remained inviting, along with the tall windows front and back. The one advantage of such an erosion of period elements was a free reign in crafting internal spaces within the fabric of the listed house.

An important early decision within the overall reinvention of the house was to open up the lower ground floor in radical fashion. Here, a warren of small spaces was converted into a spacious, interconnected kitchen and dining area that takes up most of this floor of the house; hidden swing doors can be used to separate these zones into two parts if required. This new and malleable family hub then flows out, via folding double doors, to a sunken courtyard garden at the back of the house.

This decision, in turn, freed up space across the rest of the house, devoted to a choice of living spaces and bedrooms, plus additional delights such as the library/study. The main sitting room on the ground floor was designed with a soothing palette of whites, neutrals and natural tones. Here, as elsewhere, the lack of original features resulted in new floors, cornices, skirting boards and a fireplace. The central staircase alongside was fully restored with a calm combination of off whites and pale greys for the entrance hall and stairway.

Yet Gorst also opted, along with his clients, to introduce bursts of brighter colour elsewhere in the house that help to instil a more dynamic character overall. In the library/study

The Timeless Home

Gorst and Roy designed storage cupboards and bookcases with a lacquered pea green finish, offering a pleasing surprise when one steps into the room. Banks of colour also feature elsewhere, including the guest bedroom, offering contrasts with the subtle restraint of the circulation spaces throughout.

The master suite offers the combination of a generously scaled bedroom and a substantial, luxurious bathroom alongside with space enough for a freestanding bath, a shower enclosure and a his/her vanity unit with twin sinks. The bedroom features a compact dressing unit – a monolithic storage bank with an integrated seat that not only makes morning and evening routines easier but adds another engaging feature to the suite as a whole.

Pages 162–163
The panelled study of the South Audley Street house.

Below
The top lit Georgian stair.

Right
A very bright, white basement kitchen.

Interiors and Furniture: South Audley Street

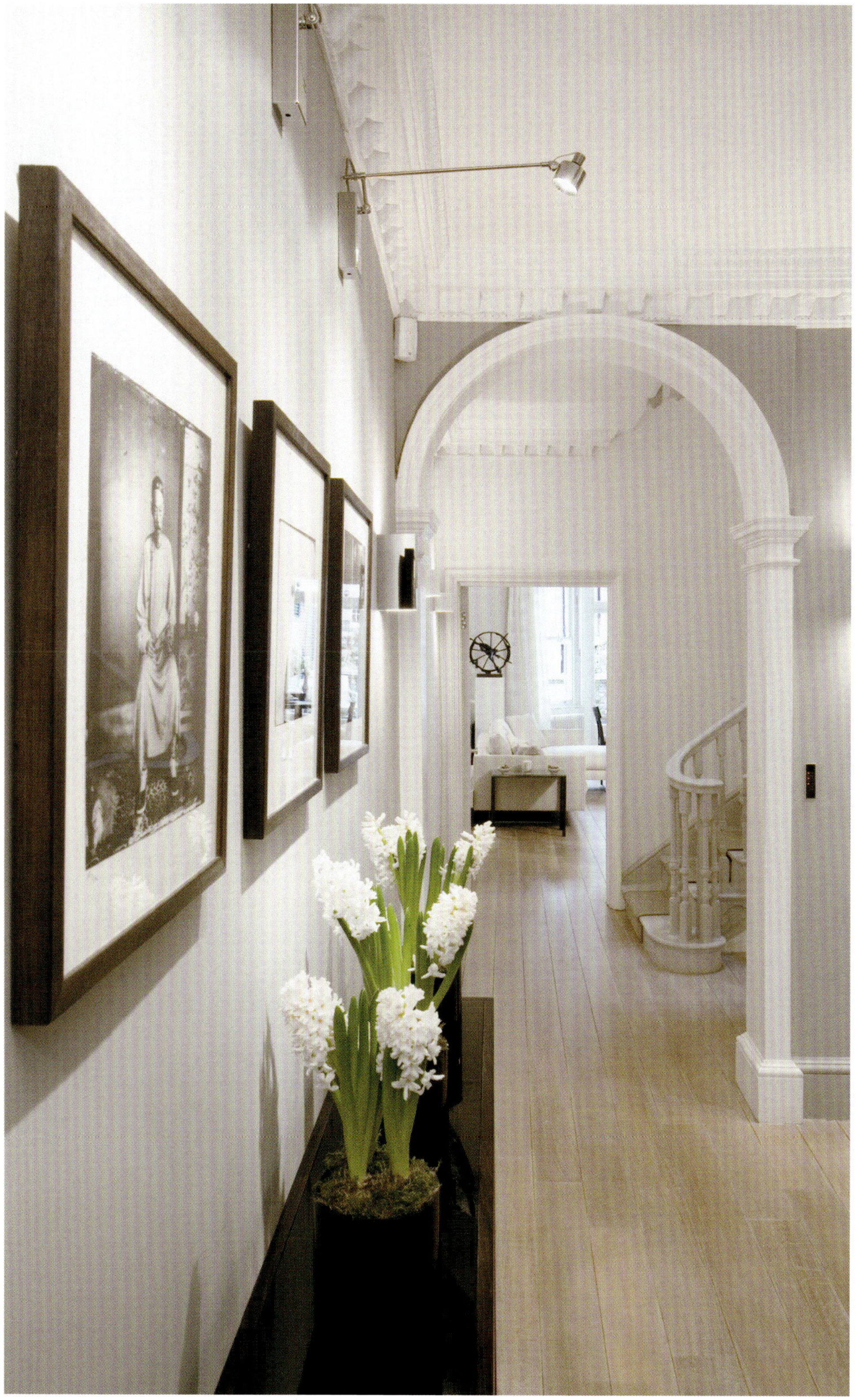

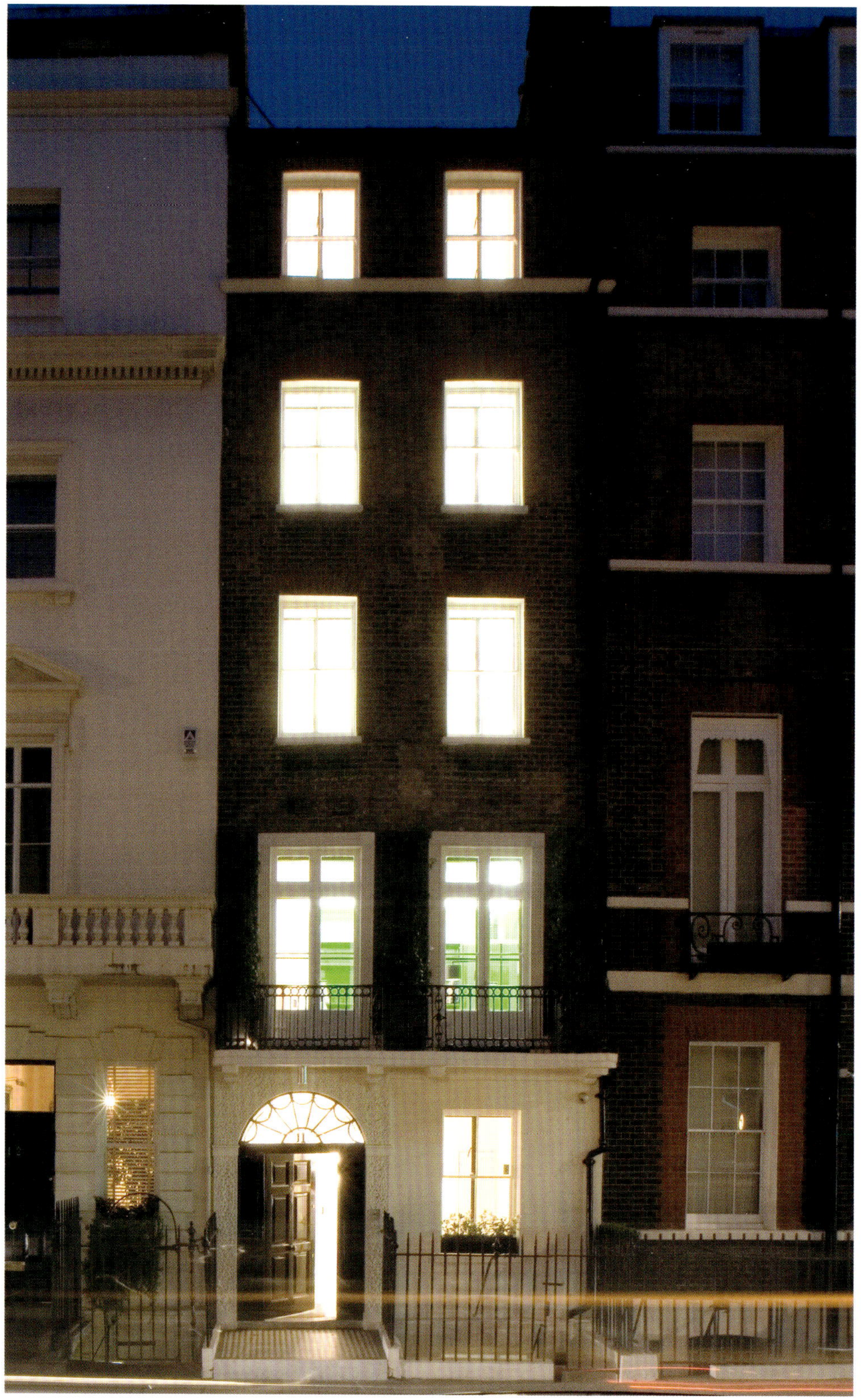

Opposite, left
From the front door to the rear drawing room.

Opposite, right
Night time illumination highlighting the gloss green first floor study.

Right
A wardrobe and upholstered seat for weary shoppers.

Interiors and Furniture: South Audley Street

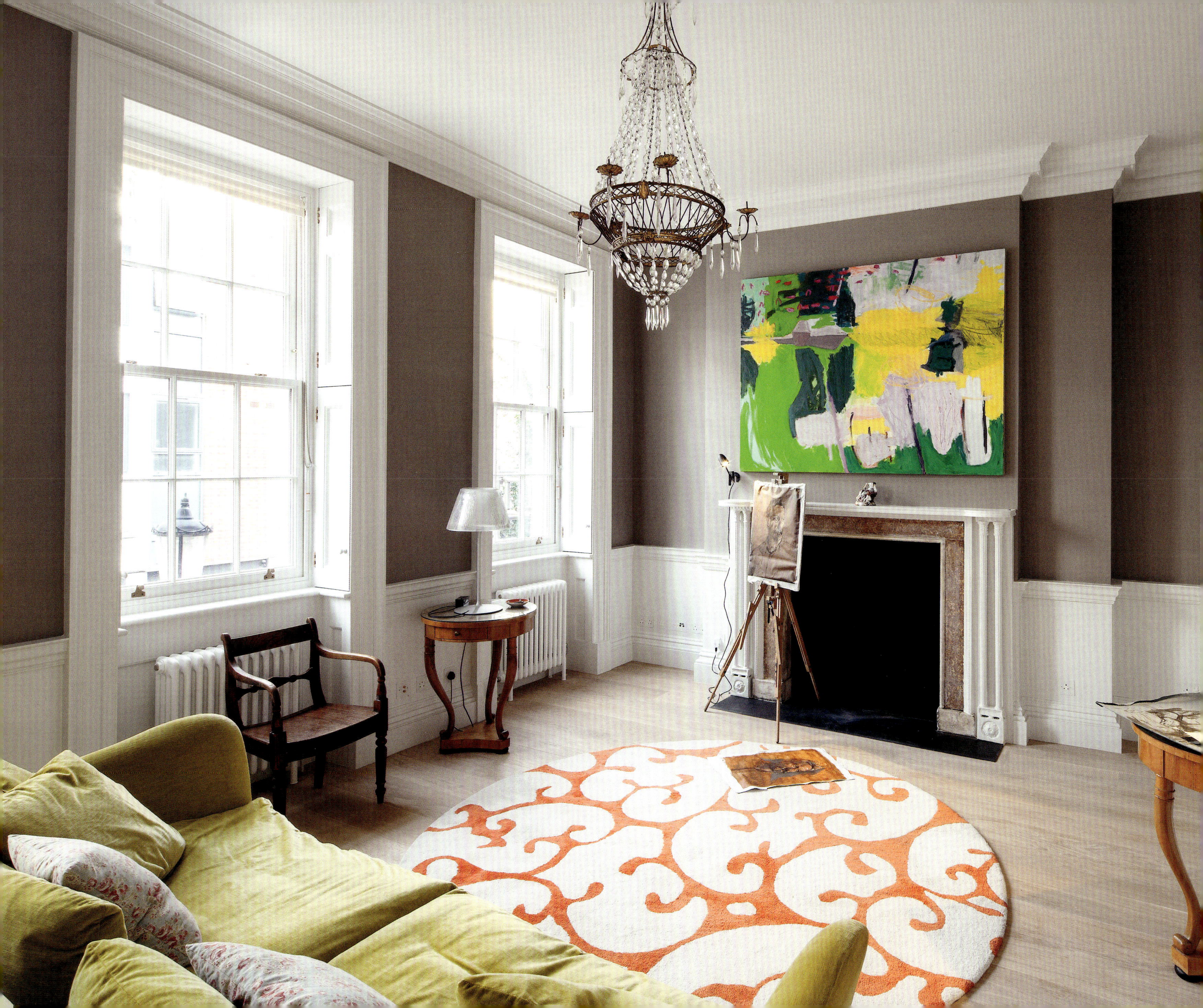

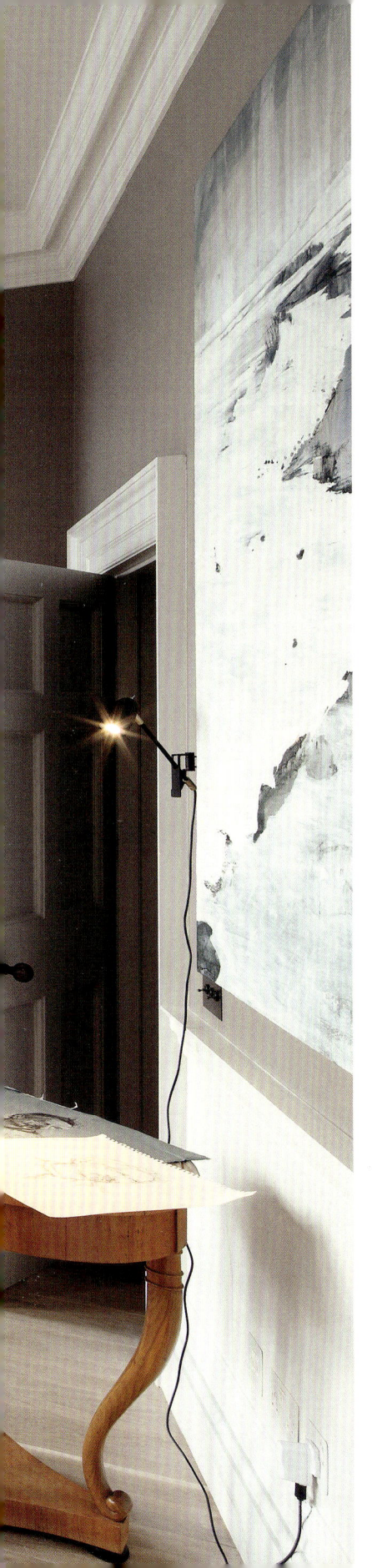

Lamb's Conduit Street

London
2015

Situated in the vibrant heart of Bloomsbury, this five-storey Georgian house on Lamb's Conduit Street has a special place in James Gorst's affections. The period property has served as Gorst's London family home for many years, with gradual changes made over time according to circumstance and necessity. More recently Gorst decided to update the entire home, restoring and upgrading every aspect of the building to bring the house into the 21st century but also lend it a degree of cohesion, unity and order reminiscent of its original period design and purpose.

Gorst bought the property back in 1993. The house had been divided up into a series of flats, with many period features lost over the years during a process of partitioning and division. The building was run down, so Gorst upgraded the flats as best he could according to a limited budget and continued to rent out a number of the apartments while using parts of the property – at various times – as his office. In this way, the house continued to have a communal character for a number of years.

Recently Gorst decided to embark on a wholesale restoration of the house, creating a fresh family home for himself, his wife and their two children. He took the opportunity to strip the house back to its bones, sweeping away the last traces of its communal past and seeking to create a single family home of character within an approach that respected the history and provenance of the property.

'One of the interesting things about the house is that it has an unusual Georgian floor plan that never really caught on in London', says Gorst. 'You have this wonderful, wide entrance hall and then the staircase is at right angles to the hallway, rather than straight on to the hallway and opposite the front door, which is much more common. So we have this very generous, broad staircase, which is top lit so that light drops all the way down into the house, and means you have well-proportioned rooms both front and back without losing space to accommodate the staircase.'

As well as restoring the original stairs, Gorst upgraded the windows and insulation throughout, while reintroducing shutters, skirting boards, dado rails, cornices and mouldings based on research and original, surviving examples found in one of the rooms.

'Because of the degradation of the house during multiple occupation for so many years so much has been changed and battered around', Gorst says. 'We had to make judgements based on the original elements that we could find and now I would say that it is an authentic mid-1740s house in terms of its mouldings, details and ornament and that gives me a lot of

Pages 168–169
The sitting room overlooking Lamb's Conduit Street, a Lucy Jones painting above the fireplace and a Russell Pinch sofa.

Left
The courtyard kitchen.

pleasure. At the same time it has gone back to its original shape in terms of the floor plan.'

The key living spaces on the ground floor and the first floor embrace the generous proportions and sense of scale that the house naturally provides. The one modest addition is a new kitchen that pushes out gently into part of the rear courtyard. With a bespoke design featuring marble worktops and slate floors, the new kitchen flows out to the hidden courtyard via double doors, complemented by floor-to-ceiling sash windows to either side, creating the feel of a garden room.

'I didn't want to put the kitchen in one of the main rooms: I'm rather against the idea and rather Edwardian in that particular way', says Gorst.

'The idea of a kitchen that is part of a communal living space where everyone can see what you are doing fills me with horror, personally, because I do a lot of the cooking at home and I like to have the radio on, pour a glass of wine and be on my own while I'm preparing a meal. So that's why I designed this extension, which means that the kitchen doesn't intrude on any other part of the house.'

Colour and pattern have a vibrant part to play within the interiors, with a hand-printed paper by Marthe Armitage in the dining room – for example – and paint colour choices from Farrow & Ball, Edward Bulmer and Marston & Langinger. The master bedroom also features an Armitage pattern paper, while the spacious master bathroom just across the landing was created by amalgamating a number of smaller rooms. A seating area set beside a fireplace gives the bathroom the relaxed character of a lounge, while bespoke glass-fronted wardrobes allow the space to double up as a dressing room. A simple frosted-glass screen separates off the shower area without intruding upon the overall sense of space.

Right
The green room, serving as library and music room.

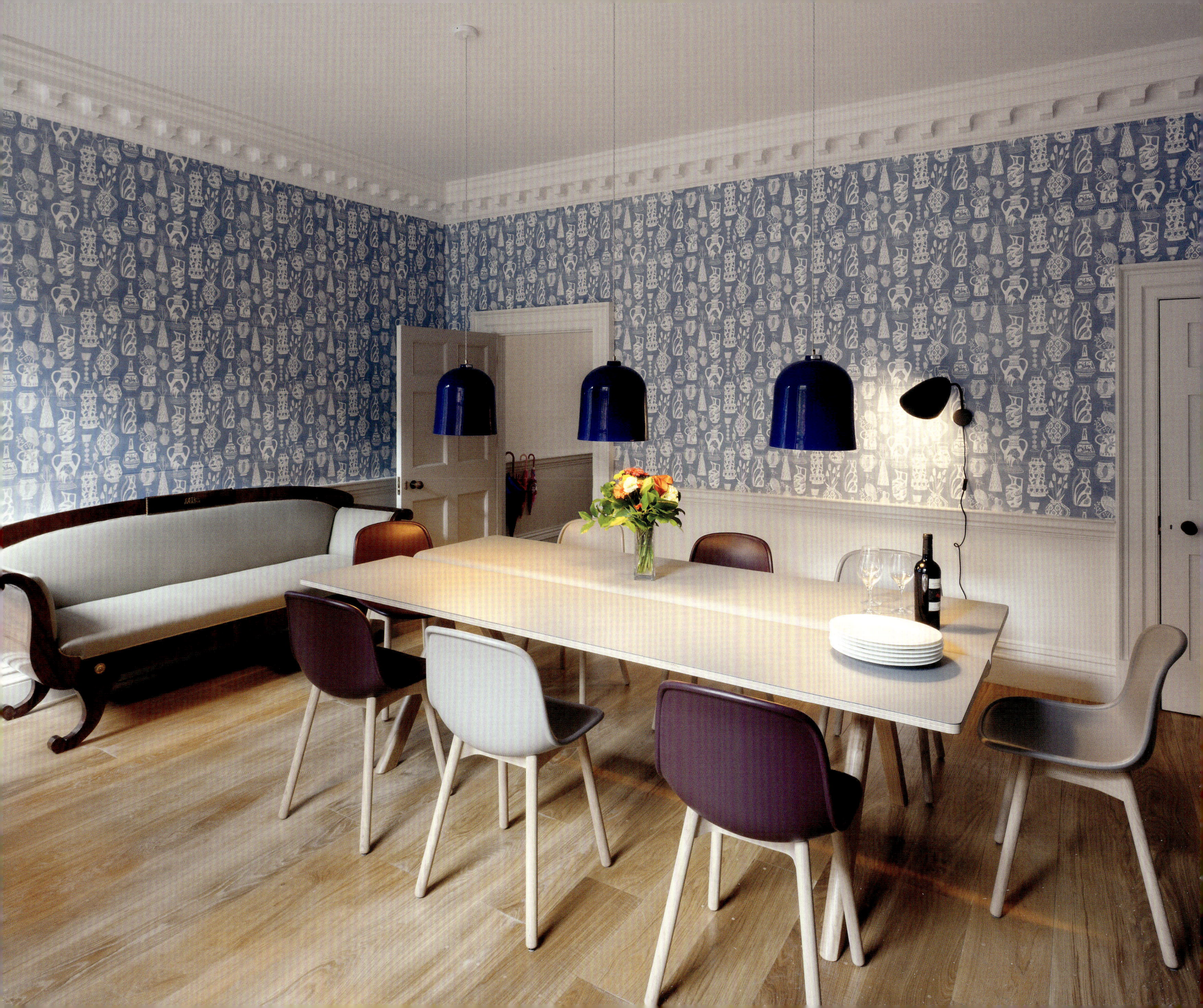

Opposite
Marthe Armitage wallpaper in the dining room with a Biedermeier settee.

Above
The entrance hall, with the staircase positioned on the left.

Above
A staircase detail.

Below
The bathroom looking through to the main bedroom.

Opposite
Marthe Armitage wallpaper in the main bedroom with a mid-century chair.

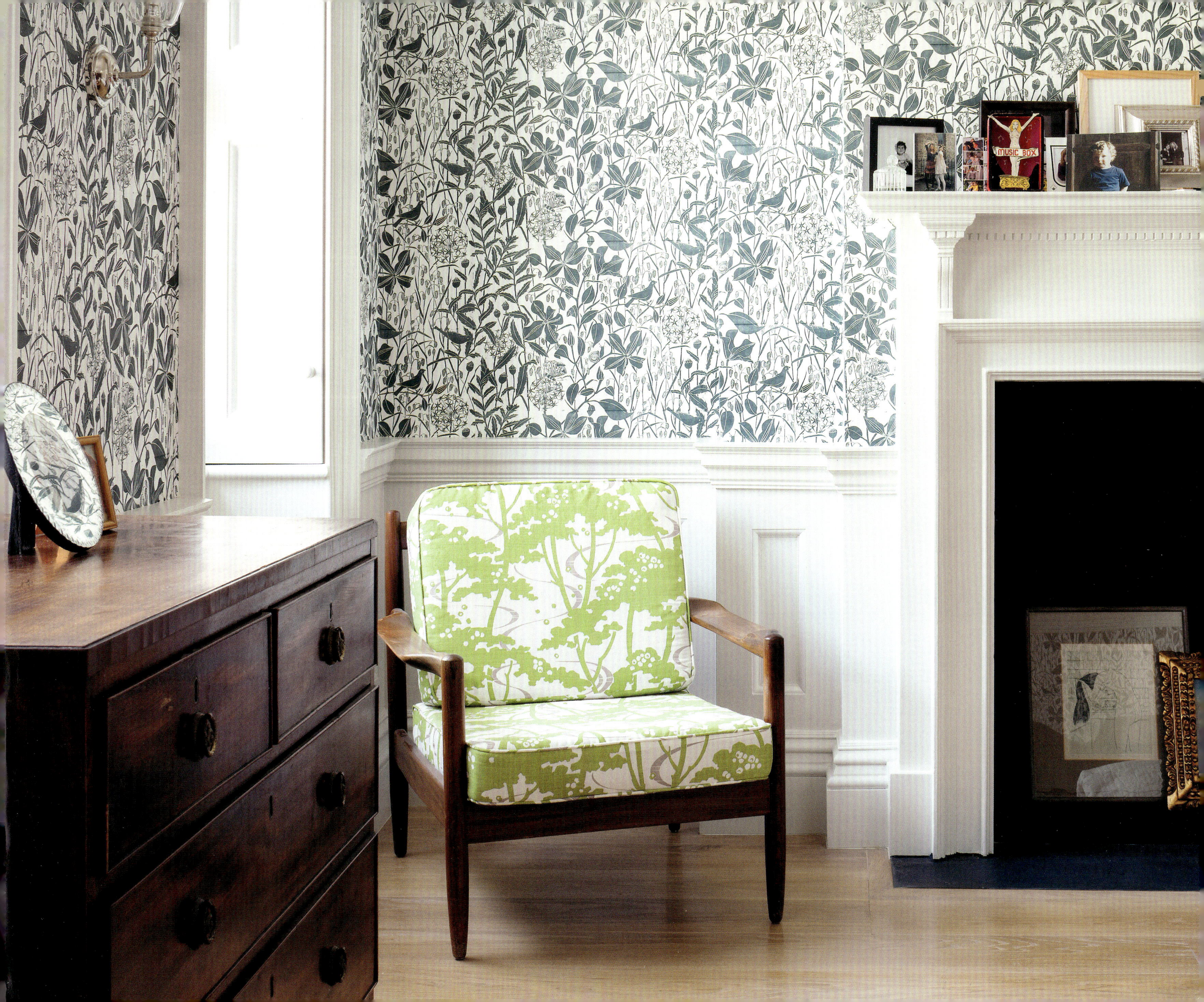
MUSIC BOX

Acknowledgements

With the exception of the early works – the shops in Farnworth, Pie Corner and Gibson House – all the projects contained in this book are collaborative. In as much as they bear my name and collectively show a singular sensibility towards materials and architectural form they may claim to be by my hand but in reality they are the product of discussions and contributions from all who have worked with me at various times. I've been fortunate over the years to have worked with some very talented architects. If I have enthused or inspired some of them then the reverse is equally true.

If one is serious about the pursuit of architecture it becomes a challenging obsession which offers in return relatively high levels of stress, long hours and low pay. However, what palliates this reality is the unbounded pleasure that comes from the shared act of creation. From first lines on paper through musings in solitary moments to discussions in the studio, the pub and the restaurant, to go on this journey from that first client phone call through to a teeming building site and the handover of a completed building is a special and addictive experience. There are vicissitudes, but we remain kings of infinite space.

My immense gratitude, for their commitment, enthusiasm and talent, goes to Sandy Rendel, Stephen Tierney, Melanie Young, Ewa Maciejewska, Lyn Ang, William Smalley, Steve Wilkinson, Sarah Graveston, Jerome Flinders, Laura O'Brien, Marie Brunborg, Pat West, Alex Doran, Zoe Polya-Vitry, Joel Morgan, Isabel Brebbia, Antje Weihen, Bhavina Patel, Andrew Humphries and, last but not least, my fellow director and drinking partner David Roy whose good humour, unflappability and calmness in the face of ruinous adversity knows little equal.

Photographers
Hélène Binet, Ståle Eriksen, Mark Fiennes, Alex Franklin, James Gorst, David Grandorge, Mark Luscombe-White, David Roy and Stephen Tierney.

Chronology

1983
Darland House, Farnworth

1988
Pie Corner, Hertfordshire
Gibson House, London

1995
Shelley Court, London

1998
Glebe Place, London
76 Eaton Square, London

2000
Poundbury, Dorset

2001
Whithurst Lodge, West Sussex
Cambridge Gardens, London

2003
Wakelins, Suffolk

2004
75 Eaton Square, London

2005
South Audley Street, London

2006
Glen View, Suffolk

2009-14
Watergate, Oxfordshire

2010
Leaf House, London
Fulford Farm, Northamptonshire

2011
Brick House, Suffolk

2014
Hurworth House, Suffolk

2015
Lamb's Conduit Street, London

2016
Hannington Farm, Northamptonshire
Sandpipers, Surrey
Downs House, Suffolk
House of Detention, London